94-12444

THE COMPLETE POTTER
SAWDUST FIRING

THE COMPLETE POTTER
SAWDUST FIRING

KARIN HESSENBERG

SERIES EDITOR EMMANUEL COOPER

University of Pennsylvania Press
Philadelphia

FOR ROBIN

Copyright © 1994 by Karin Hessenberg

First published 1994 by B.T. Batsford, Ltd.

First published in the United States 1994 by the University of Pennsylvania Press

Reprinted 1995

Library of Congress Cataloguing-in-Publication Data

Hessenberg, Karin.
    Sawdust firing / Karin Hessenberg.
      p.   cm. – (The Complete potter)
    Includes bibliographical references and index.
    ISBN 0-8122-3301-8
    1. Pottery craft–Handbooks, manuals, etc. I. Title. II. Series.
    TT920.H47   1994
    738.1′43–dc20   94-12444
                         CIP

ISBN-0-8122-3301-8

Front cover
Karin Hessenberg. *Square-cut porcelain pot with orange London clay slip. Burnished and sawdust-fired. (Photograph by Stephen Brayne)*

Back cover
Karin Hessenberg. *Porcelain twist bowl, thrown, turned, cut, rejoined and burnished. Sawdust-fired*

Frontispiece
Duncan Ross. *Burnished vase form.* Terra sigillata *fired in a sawdust saggar. Height 23 cm (9 in)*

CONTENTS

PREFACE

Denise K. Wren. *Sawdust-fired elephants, late 1960s.* (Courtesy of *Ceramic Review*)

Interest in the technique of sawdust firing is a relatively recent development for studio potters. Its origins as a process in its own right are obscure. The method is most likely to have evolved from the post-firing reduction processes of raku, which are believed to have been developed in the USA during the 1960s. This may have led to experiments with bonfire firing, using sawdust as a cheap and convenient fuel. As far as we know, there was no pioneer potter living in a remote valley quietly sawdust firing for fifty years before suddenly being discovered. Instead, a number of individual potters seem to have come upon the technique at much the same time, attracted by the effects that could be achieved on the surface of the clay.

Sawdust-fired pots have only become an accepted form of ceramics in Britain within the past fifteen years. Until the mid-1970s many galleries were reluctant to stock such work, mainly because the low firing temperature rendered the pots fragile and more easily damaged than the stoneware and porcelain to which gallery owners were accustomed. Initially, there had been a similar reservation about the fragility of raku pots, but, as raku ceramics became more widely known, galleries began to exhibit and sell first raku and then sawdust-fired work.

Sawdust firing may be a fairly recent phenomenon in contemporary ceramics, but unglazed, low-fired pottery has been made in most parts of the world for centuries. Many studio potters who have adopted sawdust firing are inspired by these unglazed pots and sometimes refer to them as 'primitive' pots. The word in this context is used as a shorthand term to describe any unglazed pot produced by low-firing methods such as those used in the developing world. Nigerian country pottery and ancient Cypriot pots, for example, have been described as 'primitive' by some potters.

The dictionary definition of 'primitive' is 'crude, uncivilized, primordial'. There is an implicit (albeit unintentional) assumption of European superiority when the word is used in reference to pots from other cultures. Because of this, I shall instead use the term 'unglazed' pottery throughout this book. As the book is mainly about low-temperature firing, and as most unglazed pottery produced worldwide is low-fired, 'unglazed' will mean low-fired pots unless specifically stated otherwise.

Pottery technology developed at different times and in various ways throughout the world. With the exception of kilns for salt-glazed stoneware, which were developed in Germany as early as the fourteenth century, kilns which could reach high temperatures (above 1200°C [2192°F]) were unknown outside the Far East until the eighteenth century. Most of the pottery produced in these Far Eastern kilns was glazed stoneware and porcelain, although a few pottery centres in Japan produced unglazed, wood-fired stoneware. These high-fired, unglazed pots comprise a tiny fraction of the world's output of unglazed pottery and, in the context of this book, are regarded as exceptions to the definition of 'unglazed' set out above.

Three of the potters featured in the book fall into this exceptional category. **Joanna Constantinidis, Byron Temple** and **John Leach** (see pages 52, 54 and 57) carry out high-temperature saggar firings using sawdust or other organic material in the saggars. Constantinidis was one of the first potters in Britain to develop this technique, and her concerns were with the surface qualities of the clay. Leach and Temple, along with many other modern potters, were influenced by the high-temperature wood-firing methods brought from Japan by Bernard Leach in the 1920s.

In many respects, potters who wood fire and those who sawdust fire share a similar outlook in that it is the random action of fire on clay or glaze that provides the qualities they are seeking in their work. It is what has been called 'the gift of the flame'.

Some of the reasons why sawdust firing has attracted so many contemporary potters are set out in Chapter 1, along with an introduction to the process of sawdust firing. The relationship between the clay and the fire is examined in Chapter 2 and subsequent chapters discuss the use of colour with sawdust firing. Various techniques and adaptations of sawdust firing are described in Chapters 6 and 7. For potters who want to try out sawdust-firing, Chapter 8 is devoted to building and firing sawdust kilns, while Chapter 9 is concerned with related fuels and kilns.

Because the interest in sawdust firing is a recent development, any published information about the technique has been scattered in the form of articles in ceramics journals or references in books about raku. It would therefore not have been possible to write an account of sawdust firing without the contribution of the potters who have so generously provided photographs and information about their work.

I hope that readers of this book will be inspired and encouraged to experiment and find new directions with this fascinating and variable technique.

CHAPTER ONE

INTRODUCTION

It is an irony that, in the latter part of the twentieth century, potters who have access to advanced kiln technology are instead working with bare clay and apparently simple firing techniques. Although all of the potters who have contributed to this book make their own distinctive work, certain themes recur in their views about their work.

Many of them are inspired or influenced by ancient pots, or unglazed pots produced using traditional methods. A perception that they share is of forms determined mainly by function, which have been marked by the fire to give their own innate beauty. This beauty is not an accidental result of traditional methods, but derives from the skill and aesthetic sense of the maker. For example, West African potters who traditionally fire their pots in bonfires value highly the artistic and technical qualities of their pottery, as do their customers.

David Roberts. *Burnished coil-built vessel with carbonized lines. Diameter 40.6 cm (16 in)*

Today, factories often dominate the production of domestic and functional pottery. The individual potter producing domestic ware by hand cannot compete with either the technical perfection of the factory-produced item or the relatively low prices that these mass-produced goods command. Handmade pottery, whether functional or not, occupies a different market. Drinking tea from a fine bone-china cup made in Stoke-on-Trent is a very different experience from drinking out of a hand-thrown stoneware mug! In India, sweet tea is often sold in rough, hand-thrown, disposable clay cups.

Bare clay feels different to the touch to glazed clay. It is warm and dry, and, if burnished, has the satin smoothness of tortoiseshell or polished wood. Warmth, not only to the touch, but visual warmth, is a quality sought after by many of the potters who have chosen to work with sawdust and related firing techniques. **Gabriele Koch** and **Pierre Bayle** (see pages 19 and 41) both refer to the warmth of earth colours – ochres, rusts and browns – and relate this to the immediate contact of the clay and the flame without the barrier of a glaze.

Several potters express dissatisfaction and even dislike of glazes and glazing. Some find glazed ceramics cold and unsympathetic,

A barrow of disposable earthenware teacups in a Calcutta street. (Photograph by Robin Parrish)

while others dislike the actual process of glazing. **David Roberts** (see pages 8 and 64) has abandoned glaze in recent work, as he has begun to feel uneasy about covering his hand-built forms with a 'layer of glass'. Other potters find that glazes do not always provide the surface qualities that they wish to attain in their work.

Contemporary potters working with sawdust- and pit-firing techniques tend to spend a lot of time working on each pot. Some of them value the slowness of their methods, which they say makes working on each piece an experience similar to meditation. Certain parts of the process are time-consuming. For instance, burnishing (polishing the surface of the pot with a smooth stone, spoon or similar tool when it is leather-hard) is a slow and tactile process. These slow stages in the making process are seen by potters such as **Antonia Salmon** (see page 20) to be essential to the nature of their work.

The direct relationship between the fire, the hand-worked clay and the form is very important to all those who work with sawdust firing. The excitement of the fire itself, the random and spontaneous patterns produced, the simplicity of the process and its inherent risks, are all factors which have

Ceremonial vessel with five necks from eastern Nigeria. (Courtesy of the British Museum)

drawn these potters to this way of working. As Gabriele Koch says, there is something elemental about the direct contact of clay with fire.

THE PROCESS OF SAWDUST FIRING

Sawdust firing is a relatively straightforward process which does not require the purchase of sophisticated equipment. The sawdust kiln is really a modification of the pit or bonfire kilns used for centuries by potters around the world.

In a typical traditional bonfire kiln, pots are pre-heated over hot embers to ensure that they are bone-dry, and are then stacked in a shallow pit in the ground. Fuel such as pine needles, wood or dried cow dung is heaped around the pots. The kiln needs to be fired as evenly as possible to build up a good heat and to protect the pots from draughts, which could crack them.

In some parts of the world, the kiln may be covered with damp turf or earth to slow the rate of cooling and to retain heat. Covering and sealing the kiln while the temperature is high enough for fuel to burn will cause carbonization (blackening) of the clay surface.

Many beautiful effects can be obtained by carbonization. This is where carbon produced during the combustion of fuel with insufficient air is deposited in the surface of the pot, which usually produces random marks of black and grey. However,

Barry Hayes. *Round vessel showing dense carbon marks. Pit-fired with fumed colours*

completely black pots can be obtained if the kiln is sealed at the right moment once the firing temperature has been reached. High temperatures cannot be achieved in this type of kiln, and so the pots are fragile. For this reason, modern potters using sawdust firing usually biscuit-fire their work first to give it durability.

Traditional potters working with pit or bonfire kilns aim for a hot fire to harden the clay effectively. The pots are stacked and covered with broken pots or pieces of metal sheet to protect them from direct contact with the fuel, which is then arranged around the covered stack. This cover has the effect of retaining heat in the stack and preventing cold draughts from reaching the pots, and the potter can safely stoke up a fierce fire.

Right: *Black stirrup-spout pot from Peru. Chimu culture. Hand-built, carved and fired in reducing conditions.* (Courtesy of the British Museum)

Left: Antonia Salmon. *Boat piece with balancing arm, burnished and sawdust-fired.* (Photograph by Stephen Brayne)

The covering layer also protects pots from carbon marks caused by contact with the fuel, which would spoil pots decorated with precise designs. It requires great skill to fire a bonfire kiln so that the pots are unmarked by the fire. In many parts of the world, carbon marks are regarded as a serious flaw on pots which have been finely decorated with slips. Full descriptions of some of these kilns are given in Chapter 9.

Sawdust is a readily available and cheap source of fuel in industrialized countries, and is a good substitute for the dung, wood or other organic fuels used in different parts of the world. It is an ideal fuel for carbonization, as it smoulders instead of burning with a bright flame.

Sawdust firing and raku are often regarded as similar processes, but firing pots with sawdust is distinct from raku in two key respects. In sawdust firing, firstly the pots are usually unglazed, and secondly they also always start off cold and are heated up by the sawdust which fuels the kiln. In raku firing, on the other hand, the pots are glazed, and they are hot when they come into contact with the sawdust. Raku pots are first fired to the point where the glaze has melted. They are then drawn red-hot from the kiln and plunged into a container of sawdust or similar fuel. Sometimes a lid is placed over the container to generate heavy smoke. This process carbonizes any bare clay and reduces the glaze, which often develops a dramatic crackle.

Right: *Earthenware pots with slip decoration on sale at Hardwar market, India.* (Photograph by Robin Parrish)

Left: *Bonfired pots cooling in the ashes. Bonfiring and pot-making demonstrated at the International Potters Camp, 1989, by Nigerian potters Assibi Iddo and Asabe Magaji.* (Photograph by Robin Parrish)

The process of raku has already been described in a number of books (see the Bibliography on page 93), so I have included it only where potters have adapted the sawdust stage as the principal decorative process for their work. Most of the sawdust-fired work that I describe is unglazed, and depends on the effects of the firing for its surface quality.

Potters such as **Duncan Ross** and **Byron Temple** use sawdust as a secondary fuel to achieve specific effects. The sawdust and pots are enclosed in containers (saggars) which are then heated up in a conventional kiln fired with a primary fuel such as gas, oil or wood.

TYPES OF KILN

Sawdust firing as practised by many potters today is carried out in the simplest of kilns (see pages 66–75 for full details of how to build sawdust kilns). A typical sawdust kiln is built of bricks about four or five courses high, on a base of bricks, slabs or compacted soil. A layer of sawdust is spread over the floor of the kiln. The pots are then laid in the kiln, partly filled with sawdust, and covered with more sawdust. Layers of pots are added until the kiln is almost full, leaving just enough room at the top to accommodate newspaper and kindling to start the firing.

In wet or windy weather, the kiln may be covered with old kiln shelves or corrugated

Karin Hessenberg. *Sawdust-fired porcelain bowls showing carbon marks. Compare the surface effects with the David Binns raku bowl in the following photograph*

David Binns. *Raku bowl decorated with a dry raku crackle glaze.* (Photograph by Stephen Brayne)

sheet metal after the fire has taken a good hold. The kiln is then left to smoulder until it has completely burned out and cooled. This can take anything from five to forty hours, depending on the way in which the kiln is packed, and on the effects that the potter wishes to obtain.

A popular alternative to the simple brick kiln is the metal dustbin. The principle is exactly the same. Pots are stacked in the bin with layers of sawdust around them. The sawdust is ignited at the top with paper and kindling wood and allowed to smoulder, usually with a lid covering the bin. Some potters use a bin with holes in the side to aid combustion. Dustbin firing is a convenient way of firing fairly large pots individually.

Another alternative, popular in the USA, Australia, and New Zealand, is the pit kiln (see diagram on page 73). This is similar to the brick sawdust kiln, except that a shallow trench or pit is dug into the ground and then filled with sawdust and pots. The top can be covered with either old kiln shelves or corrugated-iron sheeting, depending on the size of the pit.

Full details of how to build sawdust kilns are given in Chapter 8.

Above: *An empty sawdust kiln, showing the brick walls and a layer of sawdust and wood shavings in the bottom. (Photograph by Stephen Brayne)*

Left: *Vertical section through a typical sawdust kiln, showing pots supported on chicken wire*

Smouldering top of sawdust

Sawdust

Chicken wire supporting pots

Kiln-shelf lid

House bricks

Concrete-slab base

REASONS FOR FIRING WITH SAWDUST

There are various reasons why contemporary potters have chosen sawdust firing.

Sawdust is a waste product which is freely and cheaply available. Potters such as **Harriet Brisson** in the USA have developed ways of using sawdust as a fuel additive, to cut down on the use of whole wood. **Vinitha McWhinnie** is concerned about energy conservation, so one of her reasons for using sawdust is that it is a good use of a waste product.

Sawdust is also a convenient fuel to handle. Potters such as **Duncan Ross**, who works with *terra sigillata* (see page 35), and **Ruth Allan** find that the powdery consistency of sawdust makes it easy to pack saggars for controlled reduction and carbonization during firing.

Sawdust can be packed very close to the pot because it is so fine. This close contact gives a good reaction with clay bodies and slips. **Pierre Bayle**'s *terra sigillata* work is an example of sawdust and other scrap fuel, such as old roots and branches, producing beautiful surface effects in reaction with the slip.

Pierre Bayle. '*Olive*'. Terra sigillata

CHAPTER TWO

THE RELATIONSHIP BETWEEN FORM AND SMOKE

Many of the potters who fire with sawdust do so because they feel that the subtle patterns and tones created during the firing are sympathetic to the forms they make. Often they are also concerned with the tactile qualities of the clay. A smooth surface, with a shine produced by burnishing or by lustrous slips, is very responsive to the effects of carbonization and smoke.

GABRIELE KOCH (UK)

The work of Gabriele Koch is an example of how sawdust firing can be used to enhance form. Koch found herself drawn to sawdust firing partly because of the elemental qualities of the process, and partly because of the effect of the direct contact between fire and earth. She builds each pot by hand, first

Gabriele Koch. *Burnished coil pot. Height 33 cm (13 in). (Photograph by Peter Kinnear)*

coiling and then beating out the form with a wooden spoon to thin the walls and swell the shape.

Koch uses T-Material as the basic clay body for her pots, sometimes mixed with a small amount of porcelain. She colours the pots with numerous layers of thin slips enriched with oxides and body stains, which she brushes on to the finished forms. She makes the slips from the clay body after removing the grog particles by sieving. At the leather-hard stage, she burnishes all her pots at least three times with a metal spoon to bring a deep shine and silky-smoothness to the surface. She allows the pots to dry a little between each burnishing.

When the pots are completely dry, Koch fires them in a gas kiln to 950°C (1742°F), a temperature sufficient to biscuit the pieces without eliminating the burnish. She then smokes the pots in a sawdust kiln. For this process she uses an old dustbin or oil drum, depending on the size of the pot. She smokes pieces individually, unless they are small bowls. First, she makes a bed of sawdust about 18 cm (7 in) thick, and places the pot on top. She then fills the kiln with sawdust, making sure to fill the inside of the pot. Koch finds that there should be at least 18 cm (7 in) of sawdust above the pot to ensure a good build-up of heat in the sawdust.

She sets the top of the sawdust alight with a blowtorch, and then leaves it to smoulder. A lid covers the kiln loosely, to allow air to circulate. The packing, quality of the sawdust (coarse or fine) and the shape of the pot determine the smoke patterns. Fine sawdust gives dense carbon marks.

ANTONIA SALMON (UK)

Antonia Salmon is concerned with sculptural considerations rather than with making vessels. Her forms have a feeling of lift from the base, and some pieces, such as her balancing forms (see opposite) combine both a static and a dynamic element. She considers that the weight, smoothness and balance of a piece are as important as the way it looks. For her, the pieces should convey the feeling of having been worked upon by hands.

Salmon finds that sawdust firing is a more direct way of working than glazing, producing a natural integration between form and surface. Seeing and feeling the work of **Siddig El'Nigoumi** (see page 29) was an experience which stimulated her interest in smoke firing.

Like Gabriele Koch, Salmon works in a slow and contemplative way, using a range of techniques. She makes most of her work in a white stoneware body, with additions of T-Material for larger pieces to give strength and resistance to thermal shock (cracking of pots due to rapid heating or cooling). She makes some shapes by throwing and altering the form, and coil- or slab-builds others. Salmon scrapes down all of her work and refines it over several hours.

She then burnishes each form two or three times to obtain a compact and smooth surface into which she can incise, impress or comb textures. Occasionally, she applies and burnishes coloured slips, or inlays oxides (iron and manganese) into the smooth surface.

Salmon is less concerned with the shine produced by burnishing than with the smooth, tactile nature of the surface. She fires her work to higher than a normal biscuit temperature (between 1020–1100°C [1868–2012°F]), in an electric kiln, before carrying out the sawdust firing, in order to give the clay body strength. This enables her to produce more delicate forms. The exact temperature depends on the type of smoking she wishes the work to receive afterwards. Higher-fired work is more vitrified and less responsive to the smoke, giving rise to subtle carbonization patterns, while lower-fired work develops deeper blacks.

She carries out her sawdust firing in a simple brick structure built to a depth of about 75 cm (30 in), and packs the kiln with great care. Some pieces touch one another, so that the contact points are protected from the smouldering sawdust. Other pots rest on top of densely packed sawdust so that they are highly carbonized. The type of sawdust influences the smoking, and she uses a mix of

Antonia Salmon. *Two balancing pieces, burnished and sawdust-fired*

coarse and fine sawdust. She finds that softwoods tend to burn more rapidly and produce more black and flashing than hardwoods, while hardwood sawdust tends to give a much 'redder' smoking.

KARIN HESSENBERG (UK)

Sawdust firing was first demonstrated to me by Janice Tchalenko while I was a student at Camberwell School of Art and Crafts in London. Working in red earthenware, I made small, carved pinch pots and large coil pots, which developed rich blacks with an oil-spot rainbow shine in places. The method had an instant appeal because it created subtle variations in surface colour that I had found difficult to obtain with glazes, but I did not develop the technique seriously until several years after I had set up my studio.

By 1977 I was working exclusively in porcelain, and had become involved with very simple forms made by squeezing finely thrown and turned pots into elliptical shapes. I felt that these simple forms needed something special in their surface quality, and the glazes that I was using somehow lacked the life I was looking for. Some of these shapes reminded me of the sawdust-fired bowls I had made at college, so I experi-

Karin Hessenberg. *Porcelain bowl, burnished and sawdust-fired. Height approx. 15 cm (6 in)*

mented with sawdust firing in the large open fireplace in my studio.

As a result of many losses sustained in the open fire, I arrived at the firing technique described in more detail on pages 58–61. It was necessary to build a small kiln in the fireplace to protect pots from firing too rapidly and unevenly, as this was causing the breakages.

Using Potclays 1146 porcelain, which is easy to work and has a good resistance to thermal shock, I made the pots by throwing and turning them as thinly as possible. I then altered their shapes by squeezing them gently into oval forms. When the pots were leather-hard, I burnished them to a high shine by rubbing the surface with a smooth pebble, ensuring that any burnish marks made by the pebble were sympathetic to the form of the pot. I used a flat wooden modelling tool for burnishing crevices. I then gave the pots a final shine with a soft chamois leather.

I biscuit-fired the pots in an electric kiln to 980°C (1796°F), which was high enough to strengthen the body while retaining the burnish. Experiments with firing pots to higher than the normal biscuit temperature were not successful. Above 1050°C (1922°F), the fine body closed too much to take carbonization, and the effect of subsequent

Karin Hessenberg. *Double-cut twist bowl. Porcelain, thrown, turned, cut, rejoined and burnished. Sawdust-fired*

sawdust firing was to produce brown, oily smudges instead of subtle greys and deep blacks.

Initially, my fascination with sawdust firing lay in the randomness of the effects of the smoke in relation to the form of the pot. Each pot was a surprise when it came out of the kiln. However, I eventually felt the need to control the firing to achieve the more attractive and interesting effects consistently, and after experimentation I arrived at the resist decoration technique described on pages 58–61.

MEG POTTER (UK)

Meg Potter's interest in low-temperature firings developed from a visit to northern Nigeria, where the low-fired, everyday country pottery that she saw inspired her to try the technique herself. There is a rich and varied tradition of hand-coiled pottery-making in Nigeria, and as she travelled around the country she learned a great deal about coiling, burnishing and incised decoration, as well as about different types of bonfiring. Drawing on this experience, she uses a variety of smoke-firing processes for her own work.

Potter sometimes uses sawdust firing in combination with partial glazing. She fires a transparent crackle glaze to 1120°C (2048°F) prior to smoke firing. The clay body she uses for this process is a 50:50 mix of porcelain and T-Material, which provides the required whiteness while retaining the ability to withstand the stresses of thermal shock.

Like Antonia Salmon, Potter finds that the type of sawdust used is an important consideration, because different types give different colour results. Pine sawdust can

Meg Potter. *Dish form, hand-built and sawdust-fired*

leave heavy resin stains on the porcelain, while hardwood sawdusts burn more slowly and produce denser carbon markings.

MAGDALENE ODUNDO (UK)

Most notable for their African inspiration are the pots made by Magdalene Odundo. She hand-builds the pots by traditional processes using a red earthenware clay. She coats the pots with levigated slip (see page 36), and then burnishes them to a high shine. Some pieces are a dense satin black, which is produced by firing them in reducing conditions in saggars containing combustible material. Other pots, which have been fired in oxidation, are a smooth orange-red.

Magdalene Odundo. *Hand-built black vessel. Burnished* terra sigillata *slip, fired in reducing conditions*

CHAPTER THREE

BODY STAINS, SLIPS AND LUSTRES

Sawdust firing can provide beautiful and varied surface effects, or, with appropriate control of the firing conditions, dramatic blacks. However, these markings are essentially monochrome or of a limited variety of colours. Many potters working with sawdust firing enjoy the interplay of these markings on a previously coloured surface.

There are two principal methods of colouring pots before sawdust firing. The first is to colour the clay body with oxides, body stains or underglaze colours before forming the piece of work. The second is to apply coloured slips to the surface at the leather-hard stage. There is also a third method of colouring before sawdust firing, where either of these two methods is combined with low-firing glazes or lustres.

Pots are usually fired at least once to biscuit temperature to strengthen them before they are exposed to sawdust firing or smoking.

BODY STAINS AND OXIDES

This method is most suitable for white clays, as darker bodies tend to mute the added colours.

I have experimented with adding either body stains or oxides to porcelain. Adding colour to the body can be expensive in terms of the consumption of oxides, but it does have the advantage that the pot can be burnished without the risk of removing the colour, which can happen when a slip is burnished and small specks of slip attach themselves to the burnishing tool (see also page 29). Another advantage is that, whereas very finely turned pots carry the risk of collapsing if slip is applied to them, colouring the body itself eliminates this risk.

Any commercially prepared body stain can be added to the clay body. The body can be in the plastic state or weighed dry and then mixed with colour. All oxides or body stains should be mixed into plastic clay by weighing. When I was making small pots, I would colour small batches of 10 kg (22 lb) of clay. My method was to cut the 10 kg (22 lb) block into eight or nine slices, which I laid out on a worksurface. Using my fingers and thumbs, I poked holes into the slices to form little wells.

Next, I weighed the oxide or stain into a small bowl and mixed it with water to form a paste. I spread the paste over the clay slices, making sure that it filled the holes. I used a rubber kidney to clear all the colourant from the bowl. I then stacked the slices on top of each other and wedged the clay by cutting and slamming, before carrying out very thorough kneading to ensure that the colourant was evenly mixed in.

TYPICAL RECIPES FOR BODY STAINS AND OXIDES

To 10 kg (22 lb) porcelain (Potclays 1146), add:

For *pinks*, ranging from deep to pale

Red iron oxide		4%
	or	2%
	or	1%
	or	0.5%

For *blues*

Cobalt carbonate or oxide		6%
	or	4%
	or	3%

For *oranges/pinks*

Yellow ochre (Potterycrafts 3413)	10%

For *lemon yellow*

Potclays vivid yellow stain (praeseodymium)	10%

Body stains or underglaze colours can be very pale if less than 10% by weight is added to the plastic clay.

Judy Trim. *Blue pots. Sprayed coloured slips on T-Material, fired to 1000°C (1832°F) and then sawdust-fired*

Note: I found that copper oxide did not produce greens at 980°C (1796°F) unless the pot was glazed. It would be better to use chrome oxide or commercial stains if you wish to obtain a green unglazed clay body.

The mixed batches of clay should be wrapped in clean polythene and stored in plastic buckets with snap-on lids. It is imperative to be scrupulously clean when mixing clay with colours, in order to avoid contaminating other batches of clay. The worksurfaces must be thoroughly washed after use, and used polythene kept separately for wrapping clay of the same colour only. Cobalt in particular is very powerful and would easily spoil paler-coloured clays.

Since I used my coloured porcelain for throwing and turning, I would throw pots in only one colour in a day. I left the coloured slops in the wheel tray to catch the turnings of the same colour from the second day's work. I collected the turnings and soaked them down for reclamation with the water used for cleaning the wheel, so that nothing was wasted. Only when a batch of pots in one colour was completely finished and ready to dry for firing would I start work on pots of a different colour.

SUE VARLEY (UK)

Sue Varley uses clay coloured with oxides for some of her sawdust-fired pieces. The clay body that she uses is mixed from equal quantities of St Thomas's body, T-Material, and Crank or fireclay. To this body she adds oxides, either separately or in combination. These are mainly copper, manganese, iron or cobalt, but she sometimes adds rutile, nickel or chrome.

She mixes batches of clay, wraps them in polythene and carefully labels and stores them ready for use. She layers different-coloured clays in the desired proportions and wedges them together.

Varley shapes her bowls by pinching, and leaves them quite thick to be stored overnight in polythene. The next day, she pinches out the pots more thinly and shapes them. When she has pinched them as thin as possible, she leaves the pots to become leather-hard before scraping down the surface with a metal kidney. At this stage, she sometimes paints the bowls with areas of slip and then burnishes them. She biscuit fires the bowls to 980°C (1796°F) before sawdust firing them. She also glazes or partly glazes some bowls with a clear alkaline.

GAIL RUSSELL (USA)

Gail Russell works with porcelain, and incorporates body stains for colour as well as using coloured slips. She combines some of her pieces with metal after completion.

Sue Varley. *'Black Clouds' landscape bowl. Height 18 cm (7 in)*

Gail Russell. *Smoked porcelain vessel with metallic thread. 12.7 × 7.6 cm (5 × 3 in)*

COLOURED SLIPS

Many potters colour their work with slips. The slips can either be brushed or sprayed on.

GABRIELE KOCH

Gabriele Koch uses many layers of thin watery slip, which she applies with a brush.

JANE PERRYMAN (UK)

Jane Perryman (see page 64) also brushes on her coloured slips, which are made up of ball clay coloured with commercial stains. The basic colours that she uses are yellow, blue and pink. She builds up three layers of slip before burnishing the pots at the leather-hard stage using a shiny pebble and various spoons.

VINITHA McWHINNIE (UK)

Vinitha McWhinnie uses a combination of brushed or sprayed slips. She builds these up in three or four applications, before burnishing the pots several times.

KARIN HESSENBERG

When I was working in London during the 1980s, I introduced colour to my sawdust pots, using slips. I made my orange slip from London clay, dug from beneath the cellar of my house, which I combined with a Bernard

Vinitha McWhinnie. *Jug. Height 38 cm (15 in)*

Leach white slip recipe (see below). I washed, sieved and dried out the London clay for weighing. I mixed the dry ingredients for the Leach slip by weighing them into a large jar with a tight screw-top lid, and then shaking them well. I allowed the dry powder to settle for twenty-four hours before use.

KARIN HESSENBERG: ORANGE SLIP

London clay	25%
Bernard Leach white slip	75%

BERNARD LEACH: WHITE SLIP

China clay	60%
Ball clay	20%
Potash feldspar	20%

Any red or yellow clay combined in varying proportions with a white slip could produce good oranges or pinks at earthen-ware temperatures if left unglazed.

I painted my orange slip on to the porcelain pots using a small Japanese hake brush, and building it up in two coats to create an even colour. I left the slipped areas unburnished, as tiny specks of orange would sometimes detach during burnishing and spread over the areas that I wanted white.

If slips are to be burnished, try to ensure that they have a good fit with the body to which they are being applied. Thin coats of slip tend to be easier to burnish. The slip must be at the right point of dryness for burnishing; if it is too damp it will not burnish well and may smudge.

SIDDIG EL'NIGOUMI (UK)

Siddig El'Nigoumi does not use sawdust for carbonizing his work, but he achieves similar effects by smoking biscuit-fired pots with burning newspaper. His work consists mainly of burnished and decorated pots, dishes and modelled animals. He uses Fremington earthenware clay for burnishing because it is light in colour, smooth and fires to a comparatively low temperature. He applies coloured slips to this pale clay as an important part of the decoration and design.

After biscuit firing the work in an electric kiln, El'Nigoumi sometimes carbonizes it to produce subtle tones of brown. He does this by holding a piece of burning newspaper against the biscuit pot, which has first been warmed in a domestic oven to prevent it from cracking during rapid heating in the burning paper.

JUDY TRIM (UK)

Judy Trim applies coloured slips by spraying. She builds up her pots with very controlled coiling, using T-Material. This body has great strength, and allows the construction of large forms which can survive the thermal stresses of sawdust firing. Trim's basic slip consists of equal parts of ball clay and china clay, to which she adds colour by eye. She burnishes the slips before biscuit firing and then sawdust firing the pots.

Karin Hessenberg. *Square-cut porcelain pot with orange London clay slip. Burnished and sawdust-fired.* (Photograph by Stephen Brayne)

LUSTRES, SLIPS AND OXIDES

Judy Trim uses metallic lustres as well as slips on some of her pieces. She applies many layers of lustre, and often fires the pots between each application. She may spend as long as three weeks applying separate layers of lustre to decorate a large bowl, and it may be fired as many as twenty or thirty times.

RAY ROGERS (AUSTRALIA)

Rogers was first introduced to pit firing in California in 1980, and this proved to be a turning-point in his work. He found pit firing a liberating process for it gave him a freedom of expression which contrasted with the very controlled way in which he had previously been working. Characteristic of Rogers's work are his spheroid forms with scored openings resembling the gills of a mushroom (see photograph, page 32).

Most of Rogers's pieces are wheel-thrown, worked into shape and then smoothed but not burnished. The work is fired in a 0.91 cubic metre (32 cu ft) gas kiln. If pots are to be pit-fired, the first firing takes place at 900°C (1652°F), while pots to be lustre-fired are taken to the higher temperature of 1040°C (1904°F).

The pit that Rogers uses for sawdust firing is approximately 6 metres (19½ ft) long, 1.5 metres (5 ft) wide and 1.5 metres (5 ft) deep. He achieves rippling and marbling effects of colour by spraying on copper carbonate before firing. The copper produces pinks and reds. He places some of the pots upside-down in the sawdust to turn the openings carbon black. The fuel for the pit kiln is sawdust and scrap firewood, to which Rogers adds seaweed for flashing and salt to encourage orange and yellows.

He uses sawdust as the fuel for post-firing reduction for lustres. This takes place in a 0.45 cubic metre (16 cu ft) muffle kiln. His

Judy Trim. 'Moon Bowl'. Diameter 56 cm (22 in). Burnished coloured slips with lustre decoration. Smoked

clay is mostly Walkers 5B stoneware from Victoria, Australia, which he sometimes opens up with additions of coarse fireclay. If a clay body is dense or closed, it usually has a low resistance to thermal shock. Firing stoneware clay at a low temperature ensures porosity, allowing black carbonization from the sawdust in both pit and lustre firing.

ANNE JAMES (UK)

Anne James works with porcelain to make thrown pots, bowls, bottle forms and small round vessels, which she often modifies by beating with a wooden implement. The body is David Leach porcelain, which she makes up herself and to which she adds about 7% calbrite (fine ball-clay grog).

She sprays the pots with slips coloured with oxides and body stains. She adds fairly large amounts of colour to the basic slip, because colours are quite pale at 1000°C (1832°F) without a glaze on them. She burnishes the slips and biscuit fires the pots to 1000°C (1832°F). She then uses a range of resin lustres which she applies by painting, printing and sponging over resists. Pieces are often fired many times, because she adds layers of lustre after each firing.

Her use of sawdust is similar to the practice of raku. She draws the pots hot from the kiln at about 800°C (1472°F), and puts them into sawdust. For strong blacks she smokes the pots heavily, while for texture she sprinkles sawdust over the pots. When sawdust is used to reduce or carbonize a red-hot pot, it can leave a deposit on the surface of the pot which has to be cleaned off. James finds that fine, dry beech sawdust is cleaner than most other woods. She is also planning to experiment with sawdust firing cold pots

Ray Rogers. *Elliptoid, fungoid form with silver lustre. Diameter 35 cm (13¾in), height 18 cm (7 in)*

in a bin, to reduce cracking in certain forms. She says that the effects on the lustres are different from smoking hot pots, and she is not sure whether the technique will achieve what she wants.

PENNY EVANS (NEW ZEALAND)

Penny Evans was originally inspired by the colours achieved in pit or sawdust firing, but was reluctant to dig a hole in her garden. As a result, she has developed her own specific technique for post-firing reduction and carbonization.

Her work is made from a mixture of New Zealand white stoneware and T-Material which matures at 1220°C (2228°F). Evans only fires to 1100°C (2012°F), so that the clay body develops strength while retaining some porosity for glazing or carbonization. She throws her vessels, or rolls them with a slab roller. She sprays her copper matt glaze (see page 34) on to greenware and fires it to 1100°C (2012°F) in a neutral atmosphere in a liquid-propane gas (LPG) kiln. Evans also uses a glaze which she calls 'Apple Crackle' (see page 34). She applies this glaze to pots which have been biscuit-fired to 960°C (1760°F). She then sprays the copper matt over it and refires the pots to 1100°C (2012°F). This final firing takes place outdoors in a small top-hat kiln fired with

Anne James. *Bottles, lustred and then sawdust-fired*

LPG. The kiln is a metal drum lined with ceramic fibre, mounted on a brick base.

After firing to 1100°C (2012°F), she removes the pots at about 1000°C (1832°F) and wraps them in damp newspaper. If carbonization is required, she uses sawdust either instead of or together with newspaper. After about five minutes (or longer for larger pieces), she carefully unwraps the pots and sprays them with water from a hose to fix the colours as they develop. This creates a little smoke and a lot of steam.

The use of water or steam as a reducing agent for colours is discussed in more detail in relation to Greek *terra sigillata* pots (see pages 35–44).

PENNY EVANS'S GLAZE RECIPES

Apple Crackle
China clay	20%
Gerstley borate	80%

Note: Calcium borate frit or Colemanite can be substituted for the Gerstley borate.

Copper matt
Copper oxide
Red iron oxide } Equal proportions
Apple Crackle

Penny Evans. '*Flat Earth*' *pot. 35 × 27 × 5 cm (13¾ × 10½ × 2 in). (Photograph by Howard S. Williams)*

CHAPTER FOUR

TERRA SIGILLATA

Colour can be applied to a pot as a slip before firing. As I have already described on page 26, slips containing body stains or oxides develop their colour in the biscuit firing and remain the same colour after sawdust firing. The carbonization marks are formed on the slip without affecting its colour.

In this chapter I describe a different type of slip, called *terra sigillata*, which can change colour according to whether it is fired in oxidizing or reducing conditions. The reaction takes place at low temperatures, which are variable and can be at any chosen point between 700°C and 1000°C (1292–1832°F).

Terra sigillata has a very smooth, lustrous surface which resembles a glaze, and it is virtually waterproof. The name is generally used to refer to the Classical Greek Attic black-figure and red-figure painted pottery,

Greek red-figure vase with terra sigillata *painting. (Reproduced by courtesy of the British Museum)*

and to the wine red Roman pottery known as Samian or 'red-gloss' ware. The term *terra sigillata* derives from the Latin, meaning 'sealed earth', possibly because of its use on pots decorated with small pottery stamps or seals.

For centuries the secret of making *terra sigillata* was lost in Europe, and collectors of antiquities would refer to the 'black glaze' of the Greek potters. Research into the nature of this lost 'glaze' was only begun in this century with increased interest in archaeology and knowledge of ceramic chemistry. The black or red gloss on Classical Greek and Roman pottery was proved to be a slip, not a glaze, by research carried out in the 1940s by Gisela Richter of the Metropolitan Museum, New York, and by Theodor Schumann in Germany. Details of their research, which established the true nature of the 'black glaze', can be found in the books written by Arthur Lane and Joseph Veach Noble (see the Bibliography on page 93).

Since the rediscovery of the method of making *terra sigillata*, some contemporary potters have started using similar slips under the same name. The smoothness and sheen of *terra sigillata* is a result of the tendency of very fine clay particles to form a colloidal suspension. When clay is shaken up in water, all the particles become completely dispersed, but the coarser particles gradually settle out when the shaking stops. The finer particles take longer to settle, and the very smallest remain suspended.

As *terra sigillata* slips are colloidal suspensions, they are sometimes called colloidal slips. They are also known as levigated slips because of the process by which they are made. Levigation is the use of water to separate fine particles of clay from coarse ones. The clay is mixed with water and the coarse particles are allowed to settle to the bottom of the container. The liquid containing the finest particles is then decanted or siphoned off for further settling or treatment, to obtain the extremely fine colloidal suspension which will be the *terra sigillata*.

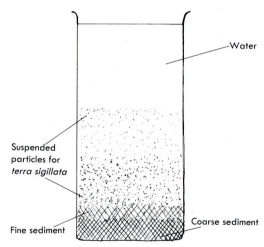

A container showing the separation of terra sigillata *slip particles using water and sodium hexametaphosphate (Calgon)*

Water

Suspended particles for *terra sigillata*

Fine sediment

Coarse sediment

In order to prevent the colloidal particles in the suspension from clumping together (flocculating) and settling out, a deflocculant is added to the water used for levigation. Nowadays this is done by adding a material such as Calgon water softener (sodium hexametaphosphate) to the water-and-clay mixture. Below is a typical modern recipe.

MAKING *TERRA SIGILLATA* (LEVIGATED) SLIP

Attic clay (or other suitable clay)	115 g (4 oz)
Sodium hexametaphosphate	2.5 g ($\frac{1}{12}$ oz)
($Na[PO_3]_6$) (Calgon)	
Distilled water	500 ml (17 fl oz)

Attic clay is a very fine iron-bearing clay, orange or red in colour. Iron-bearing clays are usually finer than white ball clays, and are therefore generally more suitable for making *terra sigillata* slips.

After forty-eight hours the clay will have settled, as illustrated in the diagram. The thin liquid containing the fine *terra sigillata* particles can be siphoned off and thickened by evaporation. Evaporation takes several weeks at room temperature, but can be speeded up by boiling the suspension until it has the desired consistency. Some potters remove the top layer of water first, and select the liquid containing suspended particles.

FIONA SALAZAR (UK)

Fiona Salazar successfully uses a white clay *terra sigillata* to decorate her large coil pots. She uses white clay so that she can colour the slip.

FIONA SALAZAR'S RECIPE FOR *TERRA SIGILLATA*

Water	35 l (9¼ gal)
White ball clay	1.5 kg (3 lb 5 oz)
Sodium hexametaphosphate	7.5 g (¼ oz)

First, she mixes the clay and water to a slip. She adds the previously ground sodium hexametaphosphate, and allows the mixture to stand for forty-eight hours. She siphons off the top layer of water and then the layer of fine suspended particles. This is the *terra sigillata* slip, to which she adds colours.

Salazar builds up the colours in layers, and each layer of slip is burnished before any subsequent colours are added. She fires the pots in oxidation to 950°C (1742°F). Although her work is not reduced or carbonized, it is a good example of the modern use of *terra sigillata* and it has some similarities of style with Classical Greek pottery.

The modern method of preparing *terra sigillata* uses manufactured chemicals, and has been successfully used with white clays. It is much faster than the preparation methods used by the Classical Greeks and the Romans. Furthermore, the Greeks and Romans used iron-bearing clays to produce their glossy slips. The black and red colours of classic Greek *terra sigillata* are produced by the action of alternate reduction and oxidation firing on an iron-bearing slip. *Terra sigillata* slip made with iron-bearing clay is red if fired

Fiona Salazar. *Burnished vessel, decorated with coloured* terra sigillata *slips and fired in oxidation*

in oxidation, and this is how the Romans produced their 'red-gloss' or Samian ware.

The Ancient Greeks would have had to use the natural deflocculants available to them at the time to make their *terra sigillata* slip. They probably used potash solution, obtained from washing wood ash. However, some particle aggregations can occur even in a deflocculated suspension and this may result in a pebbly surface to the fired slip, so the slip must be stabilized by agents which will 'protect' the colloid. These protective colloid substances occur naturally in organic matter such as sour wine, and it may well be that the Ancient Greeks used sour wine or vinegar in their colloidal slips. The thin slip could be thickened by evaporation for painting thick coats or dense black lines.

ADAM WINTER (GERMANY)

Adam Winter has spent over twenty years researching the ancient methods of making *terra sigillata*. He prepares it with rainwater or distilled water, as these do not contain positively charged alkaline earth ions, which would cause all the clay particles to sink. The more fine particles remaining in suspension, the better the slip. His method is as follows:

1 He adds between 30–90g (1–3oz) of clay to 1 litre (1¾pt) of rainwater containing either oak bark or sodium carbonate. This is then mixed well.

2 He removes a spoonful of the clay mixture from the container, dilutes it with more rainwater and leaves it to stand for twenty-four hours. During this time, the coarse particles separate and settle to the bottom.

3 He then siphons off the thin liquid suspension to allow the very fine particles to sediment. This process could take several months, but can be speeded up by adding a little salt, wine or vinegar.

4 After twelve hours the water can be siphoned off, and the remaining sediment is the *terra sigillata*.

Finer particles can be obtained by allowing a longer settling time. The finer the particles, the shinier and more waterproof the *terra sigillata* will be. This is because the particles in the *terra sigillata* are so fine that they partially fuse together during firing. This partial fusion is called sintering. Sintering in *terra sigillata* is assisted by the fluxing action of the sodium added to the slip at the beginning.

Note: Potash, which contains potassium, would have a similar effect.

FIRING *TERRA SIGILLATA*

The *terra sigillata* slip recipes did not explain how the Ancient Greeks developed the contrasting black and red painting on their pots but Dr Schumann's research revealed that the colours developed during firing. Through chemical analysis, he found that the

thickly painted black areas on the Greek pots had exactly the same composition as the thinly painted red areas. The contrast between the red and black painting actually developed in the firing.

The Greek potters used a three-stage firing process:

1 The kiln was fired in an oxidizing atmosphere to between 900–1000°C (1652–1832°F). At this temperature, the clay body of the pot turned bright red, with darker red, glossy painted areas.

2 The kiln was then sealed for reduction firing. Greek kilns had two stoking ports leading to the firing chamber. The chimney and one of the ports would be sealed, and then damp fuel and/or a bowl of water would be pushed in via the second port, which was then sealed. Under reduction, both the painted and unpainted areas of the pot turned black.

3 After reduction, a small hole would be opened in the kiln, probably by removal of a brick, to allow air to enter the kiln to re-oxidize the pots for a set period of time. The Greek potters may have used small test pieces, which could have been drawn from the kiln to establish when the colour change had taken place.

Thick coats of *terra sigillata* resist the oxidation and remain black, while thin washes and the unprotected clay body turn red again. The timing and temperature of the re-oxidation are critical to avoid reddening of

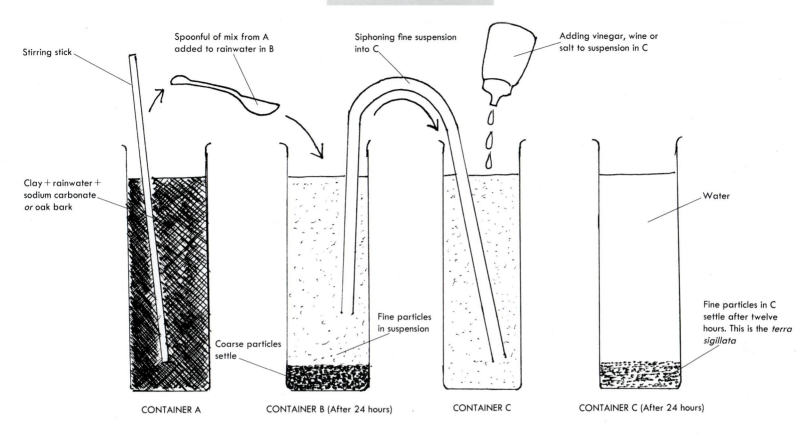

Stirring stick

Spoonful of mix from A
added to rainwater in B

Siphoning fine suspension
into C

Adding vinegar, wine or
salt to suspension in C

Clay + rainwater +
sodium carbonate
or oak bark

Water

Coarse particles
settle

Fine particles
in suspension

Fine particles in C
settle after twelve
hours. This is the *terra
sigillata*

CONTAINER A   CONTAINER B (After 24 hours)   CONTAINER C   CONTAINER C (After 24 hours)

Preparation of terra sigillata *using a traditional method. (After Adam Winter)*

areas designed to be black. Above 1050°C (1922°F) in oxidation, all the slip will become red. For further details of the chemical reactions which take place in the slip during firing, see Technical Notes, pages 86–8.

Some modern potters use iron-bearing *terra sigillata* slips, and exploit the colour changes which occur with changing kiln atmospheres. Sawdust is often used as the fuel for reduction in today's versions of *terra sigillata*.

DUNCAN ROSS (UK)

Of all the contemporary ceramics made using *terra sigillata*, the work of Duncan Ross is closest in style and technique to Attic red-figure and black-figure pots. Ross has studied the decoration and firing techniques of the

Classical Greek potters, and has developed his own firing process for *terra sigillata*, which is almost the exact reverse of the Greek firing cycle. He had been looking for a working method which was simple yet flexible, and suitable for making decorated pots. Inspired by the work of the French potter Pierre Bayle (see page 41), Ross was stimulated to make use of the research that he had carried out on the Greeks, and to develop work using *terra sigillata* slips.

Ross works with earthenware clays and his *terra sigillata* is made from a fine brickware clay from Sussex. All his work is thrown and turned. He works on groups of a particular form, and, after throwing, he selects the best of the group for further work. He turns these pots with sharpened wood and bamboo tools, which have curved profiles to shape the round forms. He carries out surface finishing using fine metal kidneys to shape and polish the inside and outside of the forms.

He coats each pot with a very thin layer of *terra sigillata* slip, and then applies several further layers of slip, gradually building up the surface by painting and stippling. He may scrape some areas to create differences in the thickness. Fine graphic tape allows Ross to 'draw' into the layers of slip to form a resist

Duncan Ross. *Burnished earthenware bowl with* terra sigillata *decoration. Height 22.5 cm (9 in)*

line when the tape is pulled away. This process can be repeated between several layers of slip to achieve a subtle variety of colour when the pot is finally fired.

When he has applied all the desired layers of *terra sigillata*, Ross gently burnishes the surface of the pot to a soft shine. He does this with a pad of soft polythene, catching the pot at the right moment as it dries. This moment is determined by experience.

DUNCAN ROSS'S FIRING TECHNIQUE

Ross fires his pots in a two-stage process. First, there is an oxidizing firing to biscuit the pot. This is usually to cone 07 (970°C [1778°F]), but can be up to 1000°C (1832°F). Different biscuit temperatures affect the colour response of the *terra sigillata*, which vitrifies earlier than the clay body. Vitrification is where the pores of the clay become sealed with glassy materials formed by the melting of impurities. Through this process, the slip becomes a sealed coat on the surface of the pot. Thick layers of slip are harder than thin layers and offer greater resistance to the carbonization of the second firing.

Ross's second firing takes place in reduction to develop the colours of the *terra sigillata*. Sawdust inside saggars is the fuel he uses as the reducing agent. He packs a single pot upside-down in each saggar and then completely fills the saggar with sawdust (see the diagram on page 49). He places the full

saggars in a gas kiln and heats them up to about 700°C (1292°F), although this temperature may be varied depending on the effects he wishes to achieve. As the kiln heats up, the sawdust smoulders and begins to smoke. This subjects the pots to an intense carbonization and produces a wide variety of colours. These range from deep carbon blacks, where the slip is very thin, through grey-greens to reds and golds where the thicker layers of slip resist the carbon.

The above technique, which Ross has developed, is very sophisticated and calls for tight control of the making and firing processes. The temperature and timing of firings are crucial for the development of colours. An extended period of heavy reduction could blacken much of the *terra sigillata*, while over-firing the biscuit might vitrify the slips too much and prevent effective carbon penetration.

Ross cleans the pots after firing and lightly polishes them with clear wax to restore the burnished shine.

DUNCAN ROSS'S *TERRA SIGILLATA*

Iron-bearing clay	1.5 kg (3 lb 5 oz)
Water	30 l (8 gal)
Sodium hexametaphosphate (Calgon)	7.5 g ($\frac{1}{4}$ oz)

Method

1 Dry the clay and weigh out 1.5 kg (3 lb 5 oz).
2 Soak clay in water for twenty-four hours.
3 Grind the sodium hexametaphosphate (Calgon). Add it to the clay and water, and mix thoroughly.
4 Leave the mixture to settle for about forty-eight hours.
5 Remove the surface water and siphon off the layer of fine clay above the sediment. This layer is the *terra sigillata*.

PIERRE BAYLE (FRANCE)

Pierre Bayle lives and works in south-western France. His work is highly acclaimed, and he is the youngest French artist to have been awarded 'Le Grand Prix National des Metiers d'Art'.

It was financial constraint that determined the direction of Pierre Bayle's work. With very little money to set up his home and workshop, a kiln capable of firing to high temperatures was out of the question. He was also obliged to use crude local clays with a high iron content. So with nothing but the basics – clay, water and a simple kiln – he set out to make earthenware pots which would have all the fine qualities of porcelain. After much experimentation, he arrived at the methods he uses today.

Bayle's current work combines throwing with modelling and sculpting. Some of his pieces are vessel forms, while others are sculptures reflecting his love of nature. Bayle never glazes his work, as he finds that the mineral qualities of glazed stoneware are too cold for his liking. He greatly prefers the warmth and life that are given to earth colours by the action of fire.

Bayle uses a white clay body for his work. He smooths the surface of each piece with a piece of sheepskin at the leather-hard stage, and then applies a layer of very thin, red brick *terra sigillata* (specific gravity 1070 – almost water). He adds nothing except soda to the clay used for the *terra sigillata*. (**Note:** The form of soda generally used as a deflocculant for *terra sigillata* is sodium carbonate or washing soda.)

The colours are produced by the natural iron content of the clay, which is between 5–10%. The shine is produced by the fluxing action of the soda added as the deflocculant for the *terra sigillata* slip.

PIERRE BAYLE'S FIRING TECHNIQUE

Bayle fires his work in two stages. First, he biscuit fires the work in a wood kiln to about 1000°C (1832°F) in an oxidizing atmosphere. This is followed by a reduction firing in another small kiln, which is tightly packed with pots and fuel. He uses almost anything that will burn, such as old roots, sawdust and pine needles. Firing takes between seven and twelve hours, depending on the wind, and reduction will vary in heaviness as the temperature rises.

Pierre Bayle. *Bouquet of poppy seedheads.* Terra sigillata

The colours created range from black or grey to pink, red, gold and yellow, depending on the firing atmosphere, the pack of the kiln and the iron content of the clay. A crackle develops in the *terra sigillata* which shows up as black lines following the shape of the individual piece. The size of the crackle can vary, and may be related to the soda content of the *terra sigillata*.

JOHN DERMER (AUSTRALIA)

John Dermer throws most of his pots on the wheel, and some of them are very large. He uses *terra sigillata* in a rather unusual way. He is less interested in the colour of the slip itself than in its reaction to carbonization and fuming (colour produced by the vaporization of salts – see page 45).

John Dermer. Terra sigillata *vessel. Height 60 cm (23½in)*

He was first introduced to *terra sigillata* on a visit to the USA. On his return he began to experiment, but he was disappointed with the results. He did not like either the crazing of the *terra sigillata* or the low firing temperature of 950°C (1742°F), which meant that the clay body of the pot was rather fragile and vulnerable to chipping. Dermer felt that this made the work unsuitable for general display.

JOHN DERMER'S FIRING TECHNIQUE

Dermer had successfully applied *terra sigillata* to almost-dry greenware, and this gave him the idea of applying the slip to biscuit pots.

He reasoned that, if *terra sigillata* would work on biscuitware, he could fire his pots high enough to strengthen them and also to eliminate crazing in the slip. Dermer investigated vitrification levels and cristobalite formation in his clay (see Technical Notes, page 88). He did this in order to establish the optimum point for biscuit firing, so that the *terra sigillata* could be applied successfully to the biscuit pots and be free of crazing after firing.

He found that at a biscuit temperature of 1120°C (2048°F) the clay body (Clayworks LGH) retains just enough porosity to allow the *terra sigillata* slip to adhere when sprayed on. Since the slip dries slowly on the barely porous biscuit pot, there is time to smooth the surface with a sheepskin cloth while it is still damp. He then wraps the pot in a ceramic-fibre blanket (this forms a kind of saggar) containing salt, copper and brine-soaked vegetable matter such as needles from the casuarina tree, and fires it again to about 950°C (1742°F). (See also page 88.)

Just as John Dermer uses minerals and organic matter in his blanket saggars to produce colours in the firing, so other potters use minerals to colour their work during sawdust firing. These methods are described in the following chapter.

CHAPTER FIVE

FUMING

Sawdust firing normally produces tonal colours such as black and grey, with incidental variations of true colours such as blue, yellow and pink. These incidental colours are probably caused by the fumes of minerals in the sawdust, which vaporize in the heat of the firing. This has led some potters to experiment with adding minerals to their sawdust kilns to fume colours on to their work. Several potters have achieved dramatic effects by this fuming process. Salt and copper salts are popular choices of colourants, as they vaporize readily at low temperatures.

BARRY HAYES (AUSTRALIA)

Barry Hayes makes extensive use of copper carbonate and salt to obtain the reds, pinks and yellows in his sawdust firings. He throws and burnishes his work before first biscuit

Barry Hayes. *Rounded vessel, pit-fired with fumed colours*

firing and then sawdust firing it in a pit. He is inspired by traditional, unglazed pots, and concentrates on making simple shapes which will not conflict with the intricate patterns that are produced in the sawdust firing.

Hayes burnishes each pot on the wheel after he has turned it. The pot is held firmly on a chuck on the wheelhead, and as the wheel spins he holds a metal, plastic or rubber rib against it. This is a very quick method of giving a light burnish to the pot. Burnishing is not essential, but a burnished pot accepts fumes more readily than one with an unburnished surface.

The clay body (Clayworks RGH) that he uses contains about 60% fireclay, and has an iron content of about 5%. It also has a very good resistance to thermal shock.

BARRY HAYES'S FIRING TECHNIQUE

The biscuit firing takes place in a gas kiln to cone 013 (825°C [1517°F]). After biscuit firing the pots, Hayes then fires them in a pit in the ground. (A diagram and a full description of Barry Hayes's pit kiln can be seen on page 73.) He covers the floor of the pit with wood shavings and fine sawdust. He then places the pots in the pit and surrounds them with

Barry Hayes. *Pit-fired vessel with fumed colours*

more sawdust. He sprinkles copper carbonate and salt into the sawdust around each pot.

Hayes covers the stack of pots and sawdust with wood, lights the fire and covers the kiln with a metal lid. Heat from the burning wood and smouldering sawdust causes the copper carbonate and salt to vaporize and fume colour on to the pieces. The fine sawdust produces heavily reduced black markings.

PETER GIBBS (NEW ZEALAND)

Peter Gibbs's sawdust pit-firing technique is similar to that used by Barry Hayes.

What Gibbs calls a pit kiln is not actually a hole in the ground. Rather it is a rectangular brick structure about ten courses of bricks high. This brick kiln operates in the same way as Barry Hayes's pit kiln. Gibbs spreads a carpet of sawdust over the bottom of the kiln and embeds the pots in the sawdust.

The colourants that he uses in the firing are copper sulphate and salt, and he sprinkles one or two cups of each among the pots. (**Note**: It is important to make sure that these minerals are lying on the sawdust rather than on the pots, because when they melt they form little pits in the surface of the pots.) He flicks grains of salt and copper sulphate off exposed parts of the pots, using a feather duster.

Gibbs then fills up the kiln with wood, stacking it directly on to the pots as tightly as possible, and laying it lengthways to prevent air from getting to the pieces. When the kiln is full, he stuffs newspaper on top and ignites it. He covers the kiln with a corrugated-iron lid.

The kiln burns down at the ends of the rectangle (where air can enter beneath the edges of the metal lid) before the middle of the top is completely alight, so every now and then he lifts the cover and rakes the wood from the middle into the burned spaces. After about six hours, the pots are evenly covered with glowing embers. At this stage, Gibbs secures the lid against draughts by weighing it down with bricks. The next day, the kiln is cool enough to be unpacked.

RUTH ALLAN (USA)

Ruth Allan uses no stains or glazes to colour her porcelain pots, which she makes with White Rose cone 10 porcelain from Tacoma Clay Arts. Instead, she obtains her colours by fuming with volatile metals, salts and combustible materials, which she places on or near the clay in a salt saggar firing. She uses sawdust as the carbonizing agent.

She throws her work, and then carves it at the leather-hard stage. She carries out deep carving with a looped trimming tool followed by sponging. She forms delicate patterns by water etching, which is done at the bone-dry stage by freehand painting with liquid wax on burnished pots. She then etches away the unwaxed areas to the desired depth with a moist sponge.

RUTH ALLAN'S FIRING TECHNIQUE

Allan fires her pots in two stages. First, there is a biscuit firing to cone 02 (1125°C [2057°F]) in an electric kiln, followed by the salt saggar firing to cone 012 (875°C [1607°F]) or 010 (895°C [1643°F]) in a natural-gas updraught kiln (Alpine HF 20). The biscuit firing is higher than the saggar firing, so that the clay will be as dense and strong as possible while retaining some porosity. A lower temperature is used for the saggar firing to avoid losing colours which might otherwise disappear.

Allan uses iron or copper wire to emphasize the carving on her pots, and enhances water-etched areas by sticking masking tape over selected areas. Copper wire wrapped around burnished vases makes black or white lines, and iron wire gives rust or orange colours. Masking tape can be used for feather- or leaf-like effects.

Allan makes small black pots with white, carbon-free lines by winding copper wire around the biscuit piece and fixing the wire with masking tape. She fires small pots inside larger pots, which are filled with wood shavings and covered with inverted bowls to keep the shavings in place.

Further colour effects can be developed by the use of minerals arranged in the saggar, as described in the following chapter.

Ruth Allan. *'Bound Earth'*. Width 42 cm (16½ in)

CHAPTER SIX

SAWDUST AND SAGGARS

Saggars are sturdy, stackable containers into which pots are placed for firing. They are made from a refractory clay body containing fireclay, which enables them to stand up to repeated firing. Saggars are used to protect

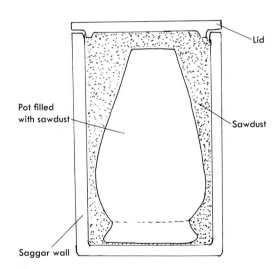

Vertical section through a saggar containing a pot and sawdust

Pot filled with sawdust

Saggar wall

Lid

Sawdust

glazed ware from fly ash and flames in solid fuel kilns. They can also serve as a means of stacking pots in the kiln without using shelves and props.

Some potters, who wish to obtain particular reduction effects, use saggars as a means of controlling the atmosphere around their pieces. For this purpose, one pot is usually packed individually inside a saggar, along with sawdust and sometimes minerals for fuming the pot.

RUTH ALLAN

Ruth Allan has extended the concept of the saggar to include the whole kiln chamber. Her saggar is a box of approximately 0.14 cubic metres (5 cu ft) made of hard brick, which she builds directly on to the floor inside her Alpine HF 20 gas kiln. She makes the saggar as airtight as possible with ceramic-fibre gaskets and packing, and seals any small cracks with kiln putty (stiff kiln wash). She then closes the top of the saggar with kiln shelves and seals it.

Allan packs the saggar with meticulous care. She positions minerals (salt, iron filings, steel wool, iron wire, copper wire) and sawdust against or near the pots, some of which have already been wrapped in wire and masking tape. She places salt for vaporization in small bowls inside the saggar, as the salt would crack or destroy the clay surface if it were to touch the pots. Salt bowls can be raised into the upper middle of the saggar by supporting them on props to ensure vaporization, as the upper part of the kiln heats up first. Allan uses about 1.5 kg (3 lb) of salt per firing.

Steel wool actually touching the clay makes strong, iron rust-coloured flashing, while if it is placed near the pot it creates a peach blush. As Allan is stacking the pieces in the saggar, she places sawdust around the pots and takes care not to disturb the minerals or wire. For dramatic blacks around the rim and shoulder of a pot, she traps wood shavings around the top using an inverted bowl. Pieces of steel wool or iron filings can be held against a pot by leaning a kiln prop or piece of tile against it. Little pads of ceramic fibre can be used to

Back wall of saggar made of large shelves

Kiln-shelf lid of saggar

Ceramic-fibre blanket seals lid

Ceramic-fibre pad

Inverted dish traps sawdust on shoulder of pot

Ceramic-fibre pad

Small pot sits in sawdust in large, water-etched pot

Small bowl of salt supported on prop

Bowl of salt

Kiln wall

Steel wool

Heap of sawdust

Brick front of saggar

Saggar wall of interlocking bricks

Floor of kiln

Saggar floor of old kiln shelves

Ruth Allan's whole-kiln saggar chamber. (After a photograph in Ceramics Monthly*)*

provide cushioning and screening between pots.

She uses less sawdust in the upper part of the saggar to allow warm, luminous colours to develop from fuming materials. A piece of ceramic-fibre blanket covers the stack, and then she places the kiln shelf lid on top.

RUTH ALLAN'S SAGGAR FIRING

Achieving an even temperature throughout the saggar is important. Allan starts the gas kiln at a medium-high setting without a warm-up period and fires it in oxidizing conditions for two hours. She then turns the kiln to high and reduces it heavily for four hours. She then switches it off and allows it to cool with the ports open. After twenty-four hours, she opens the kiln door and saggar lid, and leaves the saggar to cool for a further six hours or so, depending on how tightly it is packed. Temperature is critical to a good colour response. Cones 012 to 09 in the saggar give a good range of colours.

Allan has experimented with various minerals and adhesive tapes, as well as masking tape, to attain her varied range of fumed colours. Careful packing of the saggar and precise control of the firing cycle are essential to the success of her work.

Ruth Allan. *'Biosphere 1'. Saggar-fired porcelain jar. Burnished, tinned copper-wire lines, masking-tape patterns and trapped carbon black areas. Height 28 cm (11 in).* (Photograph by Cindy O'Meara)

JOHN DERMER

Even more unconventional than Ruth Allan's brick-box saggar is the saggar designed by John Dermer for fuming colours on to his high-fired (1120°C [2048°F]) *terra sigillata* pots. In his case, the saggar is not a traditional clay container.

The word 'saggar' refers to the *means* by which a pot is enclosed within a carefully controlled atmosphere. At first, Dermer made saggars from bricks and kiln shelves, packing the pots in vermiculite. He could mix combustible materials such as sawdust and volatile minerals with the vermiculite, and the method worked quite well for small pots. However, there were problems with dunting (cracking due to cooling down too rapidly or unevenly) of the larger pieces, so he decided to try ceramic-fibre blanket. He wrapped some pots in blanket containing salt, copper salts and brine-soaked casuarina needles, and obtained good results. The method can also be applied to very large pots.

JOHN DERMER'S SAGGAR FIRING

Dermer wraps 12 mm (approximately ½ in) hot face blanket (160 kg [353 lb] grade) around the pot, and holds it in place with 1.5 mm (1/16 in) galvanized tie wire. By altering the pressure of the tie wire, varying the thickness of the blanket, leaving some areas uncovered and using salt, copper and combustible materials, he can vary the effects produced on the surface.

Very slow cooling is essential to prevent dunting, and several days are necessary in the case of large pots. This method allows for precise control of the decorative effects on individual pieces. The only drawbacks are the expense (each piece of ceramic-fibre blanket can only be used once), and the fact that ceramic fibre can be a health hazard (see Technical Notes, page 88).

DUNCAN ROSS

Duncan Ross uses a refractory clay jar, the traditional form of saggar, to fire his *terra sigillata* pots. He packs each pot individually into a saggar and surrounds it with sawdust. The closed saggar is sealed to prevent flames or air from the main kiln chamber from reaching the pots, and this creates a controlled carbonizing atmosphere around each pot. The temperature and timing of the sawdust saggar reduction firing are critical for the control of colour formation in the *terra sigillata*. The details of the firing cycle have been described on page 38.

JOANNA CONSTANTINIDIS (UK)

Joanna Constantinidis has been saggar firing her work with organic materials for many years. She makes her own saggars from Craft Crank clay. Her saggar-fired pots are characterized by their rich, lustrous surfaces in gold, rust, red-brown and purplish colours. Her technique has evolved from early experiments both with sawdust firing and

Duncan Ross. *Burnished vase form.* Terra sigillata *fired in a sawdust saggar. Height 23 cm (9 in)*

with reduction during the cooling phase of a stoneware firing to obtain a 'blue-brick' effect on the surface of her pots. Unlike most of the potters described so far, she fires her work to high stoneware temperature at 1300°C (2372°F).

JOANNA CONSTANTINIDIS'S SAGGAR FIRING

The blue-brick firing technique did not give wholly satisfactory results, and it was a chance observation during low-temperature sawdust firing which led to later experiments with firing in saggars. Constantinidis had been burnishing her pots with a silver spoon, and noticed a metallic gleam on the sawdust-fired pots. She thought that the gleam might have been due to a fine deposit of silver from the spoon. She therefore experimented by spraying her pots with metal oxides and firing them to 1300°C (2372°F) in saggars containing sawdust, so as to achieve a lustred surface. However, she found that the sawdust burned away too quickly to give the effects for which she was aiming. She then tried other organic materials, and found that corn seeds give the best results because they maintain heavy reduction during the cooling of the kiln.

Joanna Constantinidis. *Long, narrow, lustred stoneware pot. Saggar-fired. Height 27 cm (10½ in), length 46 cm (18 in). (Photograph by Clive Tarling)*

Constantinidis sprays her biscuit-fired pots with thin solutions of metal oxides, chiefly copper and iron. She sometimes uses manganese or tin oxide. She places the sprayed pot on a setter inside a saggar. She lays corn seeds on the floor of the saggar, but does not allow them to touch the pot. She

occasionally sprinkles a little salt on the seeds.

She uses a piece of kiln shelf to close the saggar. As the kiln heats up to 1300°C (2372°F), the seeds produce a very heavy reducing atmosphere inside the saggar. In the absence of oxygen, they often turn to

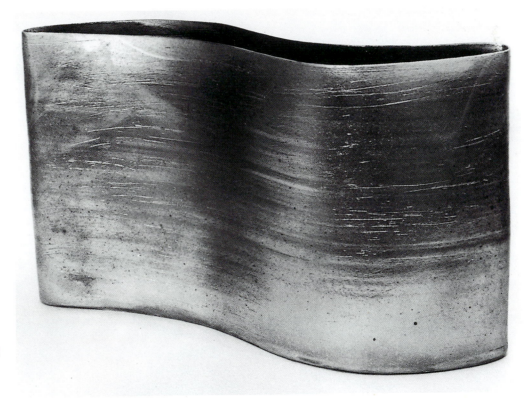

charcoal. They retain their shape, and can be used again in a subsequent firing. As the seeds have not burned away completely at 1300°C (2372°F), they continue to burn and maintain reduction during the cooling phase of the firing cycle.

The combination of the heavy reduction inside the saggar and the sprayed oxides produces a lively lustred surface on the pots in warm, subtle tones of colour. The pots may be made of porcelain, white stoneware or ordinary stoneware, depending on the effects that Constantinidis wishes to achieve. She finds that a single large pot in a saggar is difficult to manoeuvre, as there is the risk that the pot inside could tip over. She has both a gas and an electric kiln in her studio.

BYRON TEMPLE (USA)

Byron Temple uses traditional saggars, which he makes himself, to contain sawdust and a single pot. Like Joanna Constantinidis, he carries out his sawdust firing at high stoneware temperature (1300°C [2372°F]). He fires his work in a wood-fuelled kiln.

Temple has been making thrown functional pots almost from the start of his training as a potter. He first worked at the Leach Pottery in St Ives, Cornwall, and then with Colin Pearson at Aylesford, and John

Byron Temple. *Tie box with feet. Porcelain saggar fired to 1300°C (2372°F). Height 12.7 cm (5 in), width 7.6 cm (3 in)*

Leach at Muchelney. He says that he is fascinated by the unassuming beauty and simplicity of naked, unglazed clay, and this fascination led him to experiment with salt, wood and sawdust firing.

BYRON TEMPLE'S SAGGAR FIRING

Although Temple was pleased by the surface qualities of pots which had been sawdust-fired in old waste-bins, the immature clay body was too fragile to be used for functional items. He had used saggars at St Ives to protect pots from the force of the flame in the wood kiln, so he reasoned that saggars could be used to contain a secondary fuel and inhibit its combustion. At the same time, standard glazed pots could be fired in the same kiln without the risk of being spoiled by ash from burning sawdust.

Temple's saggars are cylindrical jars with cap lids, thrown from refractory clay. For ease of stacking, he makes the saggars in three standard diameters, and this provides a variety of sizes in which to accommodate different pieces. The saggar technique produces vitreous pottery with bold carbon flashing from the sawdust. Control of the sawdust markings can be achieved by varying the depth and tightness to which the sawdust

Byron Temple. *Tea jar. Porcelain saggar-fired to 1300°C (2372°F). Bamboo handle. Height 12.7 cm (5 in), width 10.2 cm (4 in).* (Photograph by G. Carr)

is packed in the saggar. The type of clay used for the pot and the saggar also influences the surface effects: the more porous the saggar clay, the more subtle the sawdust markings. Saggars made from denser clay produce darker blacks.

Porcelain pots show a greater contrast between exposed and unexposed areas, and sometimes turn delicate shades of pink and orange where the porcelain contains impurities. Heavily grogged clay bodies become more uniformly black.

BYRON TEMPLE'S CLAY BODIES FOR SAGGARS

Dense body

Scrap stoneware clays	4.54 kg (10 lb) dry weight
Soft brick dust	0.68 kg (1.5 lb) dry weight

Loose body (difficult to throw)

By volume		
	Fireclay	2 parts
	Ball clay	1 part
	Soft brick dust	1 part*
	Sawdust (damp)	2 parts*
	Scrap stoneware	6 parts

*These materials are used to open the clay body and make it resistant to thermal shock.

A material used for this purpose is called a temper.

The saggars must be high-fired when empty before they are used for firing pots.

JOHN LEACH (UK)

John Leach makes domestic, functional pots and fires them in a wood kiln. His stoneware clay responds well to the wood firing, so he glazes most pots on the inside only. Leach's black pots with a fine, wavy white line are fired in saggars containing sawdust, in his wood kiln.

He uses three kinds of saggar. He obtains one type from a commercial saggar-maker, Acme Marls in Stoke-on-Trent (see the List of Suppliers on page 92); others come from China; and some he makes himself using flowerpots covered with batt lids. He finds that pots fired in the Chinese saggars tend to have a colour gradient, being black near the bottom and fading through grey to a biscuity colour near the top. Leach thinks that this is because the Chinese saggars have rather loose lids, and are made from an open clay body.

Pots fired in his own flowerpot saggars made from his standard stoneware body develop more black. This is because the

standard body is denser than normal saggar clays and, in addition, these saggars are very well sealed except for a pin-prick hole. This hole may have some influence on where the white line develops on the pot.

JOHN LEACH'S SAGGAR FIRING

Leach places a single pot in each saggar, and then partly fills the saggar with sawdust. The white line forms at the level of the sawdust contour. He is unsure of the exact chemical process which takes place, but he has observed that the pot is very black and smooth where it has been buried in the sawdust. Above the white line, the colour is greyer and the pot is not as smooth. Sometimes he will pack a pot upside-down in the saggar to produce a rich, black top.

Leach uses hardwood sawdust in his saggars, which he obtains from a local college of furniture. This is mainly ash, beech and oak. Very fine, dusty sawdust is not suitable. He prefers sawdust from hardwood, as he finds that sawdust from softwood produces resins and burns with a smoky flame. Hardwood has a higher calorific value than softwood, and burns with a shorter, cleaner flame. Although he uses hardwood sawdust, he fires the wood kiln with softwood – mainly larch and pine.

John Leach. *Pitchers saggar-fired to 1300°C (2372°F)*

CHAPTER SEVEN

RESIST TECHNIQUES IN FIRING

Resist is a technique in which a material covers part of a pot to prevent a decorative coating, such as slip, from reaching the surface of the pot. Two of the best-known resist processes are paper resist, where paper stencils are used for slip decoration, and wax resist, which is used in glazing with two or more layers of glaze.

One of the attractions of sawdust firing is the contrast between black and white combined with random cloudy, smoky patterns. Random smoky patterns are not always interesting, however, and dark patches of carbon can obscure the colours of clay bodies or slips. For this reason, some potters have devised techniques to control the areas where carbonization occurs on the surface of pots.

KARIN HESSENBERG

When I first thought of my 'carbonization-resist' method, I was interested in obtaining patterns on the pots. The idea came to me from Japanese Bizen pots, which were decorated with a pattern of a full moon and

Karin Hessenberg. *Porcelain vase form, burnished and sawdust-fired, and showing carbonization resist and grass 'print'*

band of cloud. These pots were fired in wood kilns, in which the clay surface reacted with fly ash to form a glaze.

The 'moon' was a pale circle crossed by one or two fine red bands, possibly made by sticking a circular pad of refractory clay and some rice straws against the surface of the pot. Alternatively, these patches may have been formed where straw was placed between the pots to pad them where they touched in the kiln, the 'moon' effect being the result of these contact points. The clay pad protected the area of the 'moon' circle from glazing by the flying ash, and the rice straws burned to produce the red bands.

KARIN HESSENBERG'S RESIST-FIRING TECHNIQUE

It occurred to me that a similar technique could be used in sawdust firing. My first experiments were with dry grass stalks placed against the surface of a porcelain pot by means of a thinly rolled-out circle of fresh clay. The patch covered by the circle was protected from carbonization in the sawdust kiln. The experiments were successful: the

grass burned under the pad to form a carbon print of itself against the white porcelain.

This idea led to pattern-making using strips of paper to form zig-zag stripes, which followed the form of the cut-and-altered pots that I was making. I was able to tear across the paper strips to form diamond-shaped spots, which I arranged randomly on a thin pad of fresh clay.

I cut the clay pad with a knife to fit the shape of the pot, so that there was a clear boundary between protected and unprotected areas of the pot. Biscuited clay absorbs water from fresh clay and dries it out quickly. I therefore had to place the clay pad on to the pot immediately before packing it into the sawdust kiln, or it would slide off.

The clay pad has to be cut from a *thin* slab of clay in order to prevent the paper pieces or dried grass from absorbing moisture from the clay, and also to allow sufficient penetration of heat to burn the paper. However, thick clay pads can be used on their own to make resist marks on the clay body which contrast with the uncovered, carbonized areas of the pot.

Karin Hessenberg. *Porcelain jug form with carbonization resist and paper 'print'.* (Photograph by Stephen Brayne)

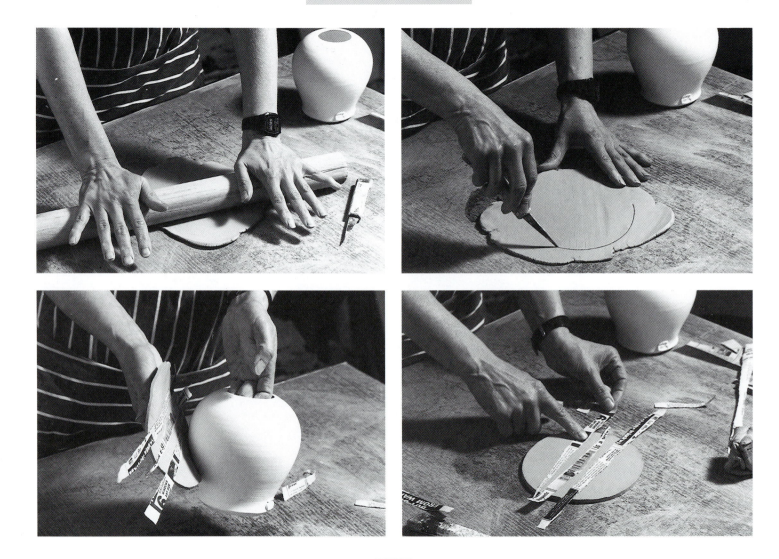

Facing page, clockwise from top left:

The carbonization resist process. Rolling out fresh clay to make a thin pad

Cutting out a circular pad

Placing torn paper strips across the pad

Applying the pad and paper strips to the side of a pot

Right: *Packing the pot and its pad into the sawdust kiln. Some sawdust is put inside the pot to carbonize the interior. The paper strips burn and 'print' their own shape as carbon marks. See the photograph on page 59 for paper marks. (*Photographs by Stephen Brayne*)*

SUSAN HALLS (UK)

Susan Halls uses a similar method of clay resist for making stripes and other marks on her sawdust-fired sculptures. She is well-known for her animal sculptures, and has recently become interested in the interpretation of everyday objects such as clothes, shoes and cars.

She makes the sculptures from soft slabs of clay, to which she adds 20% paper pulp and 4% chopped nylon fibre. This gives flexibility and strength at the making stage, and also makes the larger pieces very light when finished, because the paper and nylon burn away during the firing. The clay body is a mixture of equal parts of the following:

T-Material
Craft Crank clay
White stoneware

SUSAN HALLS'S RESIST-FIRING TECHNIQUE

Halls usually biscuit fires her sculptures to 1000°C (1832°F). If she wants subtle greys and browns, she sawdust fires her work, but for denser blacks she heats the work to 850°C (1562°F) in a raku kiln and then plunges it into very fine sawdust. Areas to be white (or

whatever colour the clay body is) are masked off with very groggy clay before firing to 850°C (1562°F). This clay resist is raw, so care has to be taken to fire the raku kiln slowly to avoid the clay exploding. During the reduction stage in the sawdust, the smoke cannot penetrate this groggy clay.

Halls has also evolved a method of smoking pieces with sawdust to achieve a range of colours, including 'nicotine' yellow, browns, blue-greys and blacks. Her sawdust-firing chamber can be seen on page 72.

Susan Halls. *'Stripey-toed Boot', 1993. Paper with clay, sawdust-fired with clay resist. Height 23 cm (9 in), length 23.5 cm (9¼ in), width 11 cm (4¼ in)*

Jane Perryman. *A group of jugs with slip and masking-tape resist patterns. Sawdust-fired*

JANE PERRYMAN

Jane Perryman makes hand-built, smoke-fired vessel forms which are mostly bowls, vases and jugs. She uses a combination of hand-building techniques such as press-moulding, slabbing and coiling. Her recent work is all coiled. The clay is a 3:1 mix of T-Material and porcelain, covered with a ball-clay slip which is coloured with commercial stains. She paints three layers of slip on to the pot at the leather-hard stage, and when it is sufficiently dry burnishes the pot with a shiny pebble and a variety of spoons.

JANE PERRYMAN'S RESIST-FIRING TECHNIQUE

Perryman first biscuit fires the coloured pots to 980°C (1796°F) in a 0.14 cubic metre (5 cu ft) gas kiln. She sometimes burns organic material inside and underneath the pots, and this can leave interesting markings. When the biscuit firing is complete, she uses masking tape to build up patterns on the pot. She then paints the whole surface with a clay slurry/slip. She then fires the pot in sawdust. The tape burns away, exposing the parts beneath it to the smoke, while the slurry/slip acts as a resist against the smoke. After the smoke firing, the resist slurry has to be scraped off the surface of the pot. The pot is washed and finished with a coat of beeswax polish.

Perryman's sawdust kiln consists of loosely stacked house bricks, and she can change the shape and size of the kiln to suit the size and quantity of pots she is firing. She places the pots on approximately 7.5 cm (3 in) of sawdust, and then packs more sawdust around and on top of the pots. She lights the kiln from the top and covers it with a metal sheet. In order to avoid excess smoke, Perryman cuts down the firing time by using coarse sawdust (almost wood shavings), which burns much faster than fine sawdust.

DAVID ROBERTS (UK)

David Roberts feels that, although utility may be one consideration, this is not the main reason for an individual in the industrialized world to make ceramics today. He makes the important point that ceramics which are handmade by individual potters should be regarded as an expressive art form.

The emphasis in Roberts's work is on form, volume and circularity. He hand-builds his vessels by coiling, and this gives him great control over the form. He is well-known for his inventive use of his white crackle raku glaze, but he views the term 'raku' in the widest sense as 'drawing pots from the kiln and doing something with them'. He has recently been producing work which is completely bare of glaze. These pots have a pattern of dark, smoked lines marked out against the white clay body. Some of these lines follow the crackle of the raku glaze, while others follow lines drawn into the resist (see photograph on page 8).

Roberts uses two clay bodies to build his pots:

St Thomas's white stoneware plastic clay	2.5 kg (5½ lb)
plus	
Dry grog	1.5 kg (3 lb 5 oz)
T-Material	50%
Porcelain	50%

He builds up the pots from a narrow base using extruded coils. When leather-hard, he covers the pots with several layers of fine, levigated slip made from ESVA ball clay, which fires ivory-white. (See page 36 for information on the preparation of levigated slips.) He burnishes the slip between each layer to give a deep, silky sheen. The slip provides a smooth, fine surface which is more responsive to smoking marks than the coarser clay body from which the pots are built. The coarse body is necessary to give strength and resistance to thermal shock.

DAVID ROBERTS'S RESIST-FIRING TECHNIQUE

Roberts biscuit fires the prepared pots to Orton cone 06 (1020°C [1868°F]) in an electric kiln. After the biscuit firing, he sprays the pots with a thick layer (up to 3 mm [⅛ in]) of resist slip, which prevents the final layer of glaze from fixing to the pot. He tests the resist slip with a pin to ensure that it is the correct thickness, and, when it is thoroughly dry, sprays the pot with a raku crackle glaze.

Roberts then raku fires the pot in a propane-gas top-hat kiln to about 850–900°C (1562–1652°F). When the glaze is thoroughly melted, he draws the pot from the kiln and allows it to cool rapidly for 10–30 seconds to generate pronounced crazing. He then places the pot carefully into sawdust in a purpose-built bin and leaves it to smoke and cool for approximately one hour. When the pot is removed from the reduction bin, the upper layer of glaze and slip falls off the pot, revealing the pattern of crackle. The smooth surface of the pot provided by the burnished, levigated slip helps to prevent the later coat of resist slip adhering too firmly to the pot.

Roberts's recent pots are decorated with simple curved and linear patterns incised into the upper glaze layer before raku firing. The final process is to clean off any residual resist slip, and then to seal the surface of the pot with wax polish made from natural materials such as beeswax.

DAVID ROBERTS'S RECIPES

Levigated slip (see page 36)
ESVA ball clay
plus
Small percentages of glaze stain if desired

Resist slip
China clay	3 parts (vol)
Flint	2 parts (vol)
Copper oxide	10%

Raku crackle glaze
High-alkali frit	45%
Borax frit	45%
China clay	10%

The resist methods used in sawdust firing fall into two main categories. These methods can be modified or adapted as desired. The categories are:

1 Shaped clay pads (Karin Hessenberg, Susan Halls)
2 Thick slip: either full cover or on selected areas (Jane Perryman, David Roberts)

Within these basic resist categories, carbon patterns can be made using the following techniques:

(a) 'Printing' by combustion of paper or organic material under a pad of clay (Karin Hessenberg)
(b) Burning masking tape and slurry resist (Jane Perryman)
(c) Drawing through slip (David Roberts)

CHAPTER EIGHT

SAWDUST KILNS

Sawdust kilns are generally very simple structures. There are three basic types:

1 Brick kilns
2 Pit kilns
3 Bin kilns

Of these types of kiln, brick and pit kilns are sometimes regarded as being the same. 'Pit kiln' can refer to a structure of bricks built above the ground.

BRICK KILNS

Brick kilns are probably the easiest type of kiln to make and fire. They are very adaptable, in that they can be tailored to fit the size and quantity of pots to be fired at any one time. They can be built to accommodate a single large piece, or many small pots.

Brick kilns do not need a large hole to be dug in the ground, which is an advantage to those potters who have only a small space available. Brick kilns can be designed for fast or slow sawdust firing by adjusting the gaps between the bricks to allow controlled entry of air into the kiln.

KARIN HESSENBERG

My sawdust kiln is roughly circular in shape and is built of old kiln bricks. Ordinary house bricks would do just as well. The kiln is built on to a floor of kiln bricks, and is about four courses of bricks high. The oval shape means that the bricks are in contact only on the inside corners, leaving narrow gaps for air. Gaps can be enlarged by widening the kiln if required. I fire my sawdust kiln fairly quickly – normally in about five or six hours – and I use no lid unless it is raining or very windy.

Before packing the pots into the kiln, I lay a bed of screwed-up newspaper and sawdust on the bottom of the kiln. It is important to make sure that this bed is just thick enough to pad the pots, and to ensure that there is sufficient fuel to burn at the bottom. If the bed is too thick, the pots could drop sharply as the paper burns and shrinks to ash.

I like the mottled effects and subtle yellows, pinks and blue-greys obtainable with fast sawdust firing, so I only cover the pots with a few millimetres ($\frac{1}{4}$ in) of sawdust before stacking in the next layer of pots. This thin layer of sawdust prevents pots from suddenly dropping on to each other as the sawdust burns. I make sure that handfuls of fine sawdust – which will create dense black marks – are in contact with each pot, before surrounding the pots with coarser shavings. I partly fill each pot with sawdust to carbonize the inside, but I allow enough air space to ensure combustion.

When the kiln is full of pots, I put a thick layer of sawdust and shavings on top, and then use crumpled newspaper and kindling wood to light the fire. I light the kiln at several points around the top to encourage even burning down the kiln. If the fuel is damp, I sometimes use a little paraffin (kerosene) to start the firing. A cupful sprinkled over the sawdust is usually sufficient. **Note:** NEVER use petrol (gasoline) for this purpose, as the vapour is inflammable and it will ignite explosively.

The kiln fires quickly, and if it has been started early enough it is sometimes possible to unpack it the same evening. However, it is usually safer to leave unpacking until the following day, to avoid dunting due to sudden cold draughts on a hot pot.

VERTICAL SECTION THROUGH KILN

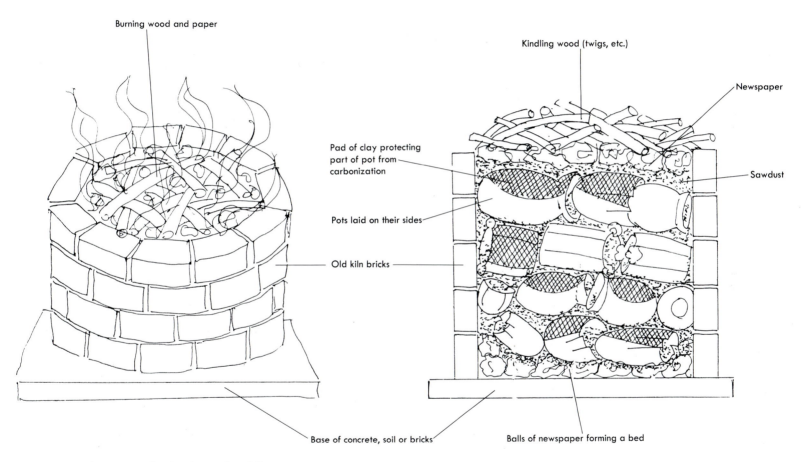

Burning wood and paper

Kindling wood (twigs, etc.)

Newspaper

Pad of clay protecting part of pot from carbonization

Sawdust

Pots laid on their sides

Old kiln bricks

Base of concrete, soil or bricks

Balls of newspaper forming a bed

Karin Hessenberg's circular brick sawdust kiln

Karin Hessenberg. *'Bridge Pot'. Thrown and slab-built. T-Material and porcelain. Sawdust-fired.* (Photograph by Stephen Brayne)

The pots at the top of the kiln tend to develop brown colours with occasional flashes of yellow or pink, while near the bottom, where heat has had time to accumulate, there are more black-and-white contrasts. I have found that slow firings with a lot of fine sawdust tend to produce more even results and denser blacks. Kilns containing a mix of sawdust and wood shavings, which burn down more quickly, may produce greater variations in colour.

Many potters who sawdust fire prefer a much slower firing time. Sue Varley, for example, fires her brick sawdust kiln for about twenty-four hours.

MEG POTTER

For Meg Potter, the ratio of pots to sawdust is an important consideration – more pots mean less sawdust and therefore less interesting carbon markings, and vice versa. She packs her sawdust kiln with plenty of sawdust, using at least 10–15 cm (4–6 in) around each pot to create the maximum surface area of smouldering sawdust in direct contact with the pot. She ignites her kiln at the top, and allows it to smoulder until all the sawdust has burned away. This takes about forty-eight hours for the best results. The kiln is then allowed to cool for a further twenty-four hours.

As Potter uses thick layers of sawdust, she places sheets of chicken wire across courses of bricks to prevent pots falling as the sawdust burns down. Her kiln is a rectangle of ordinary house bricks built on a concrete base. She rebuilds it after each firing to fit individual pots.

Meg Potter. *Jug forms. Sawdust-fired*

Judy Trim. *Tall vessel. Height 53.3 cm (21 in). T-Material sprayed with slip. Incised, painted decoration at the top. Sawdust-fired*

JUDY TRIM

Judy Trim's 'brick kiln' is, in fact, made of breeze blocks. As the series of photographs shows, the firing takes place without a lid until all the flames have died down. She then covers the kiln with a lid and seals the sides with soft clay to prevent any draughts reaching the pots. As Judy Trim's pots are large, they are particularly vulnerable to draughts and require slow cooling.

Judy Trim packing and firing her sawdust kiln. Filling the kiln with fine sawdust

Setting light to the top of the kiln

When the kiln has burned down, the top is covered with a lid and the sides are sealed with soft clay to exclude draughts

SUSAN HALLS

Susan Halls has gone a stage further in designing a brick sawdust kiln for her very individual animal sculptures. Instead of covering each piece with sawdust, as in a conventional kiln, she suspends it above a bed of smouldering sawdust.

The sculpture is supported at three points for maximum stability. The supports consist of pillars of brick with a ceramic-fibre cushion on top. The points at which the sculpture touches the support remain unsmoked, giving rise to some interesting visual effects. The colours from the smoke vary depending on how long the firing lasts. On the pale clay body used by Halls, yellows develop in the early stages of firing. Blue-grey, sable brown and a rich charcoal black can also be achieved by longer smoking.

PIT KILNS

Pit kilns are closely related to brick kilns. They have two very useful characteristics: there are no gaps in the walls to allow in draughts, and the earth sides of the pit ensure excellent accumulation and conservation of heat during the firing. Pits can be made as wide and as long as may be required; some are even dug as trenches.

Animal sculpture

Smoke

Ceramic-fibre pad on top of pillar

Brick pillar supporting sculpture

Kiln-shelf lid

Wall formed by kiln shelves

Smouldering sawdust

Ground level

Susan Halls's smoking kiln

BARRY HAYES

The depth of the pit is an important factor, and Barry Hayes finds that 1 metre (3 ft 4 in) is the optimum. If the pit is too deep, it is difficult to pack the pots. On the other hand, if it is too shallow the firing will oxidize too much. His kiln is about 4 metres (13 ft) long by 1 metre (3 ft 4 in) wide by 1 metre (3 ft 4 in) deep.

Hayes lays his pots on a bed of fine sawdust and wood shavings, as described on page 46. He uses wood offcuts from a timber yard to start the kiln. These burn for longer than kindling twigs, and so ensure that the fire is maintained to keep the sawdust smouldering. He covers the kiln with a corrugated-iron lid and leaves it to burn slowly for three hours.

After this time, he opens the lid gradually and stokes the kiln as necessary. This process continues for another eight hours or so, and then, as the embers burn down, he slowly closes the pit kiln again. He then leaves it for twenty-four hours to cool. Hayes finds that fine sawdust burns slowly and produces deep blacks, in contrast to the browns produced by faster-burning shavings.

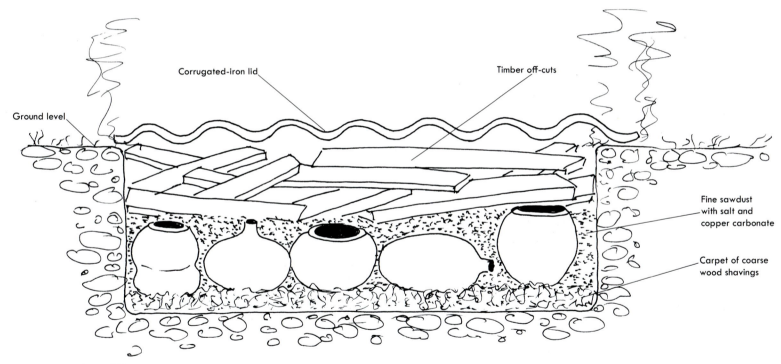

Corrugated-iron lid

Timber off-cuts

Ground level

Fine sawdust with salt and copper carbonate

Carpet of coarse wood shavings

Barry Hayes's pit kiln

RAY ROGERS

Ray Rogers also fires in a pit kiln. His pit is a little deeper, 1.5 metres (approximately 5 ft). He places the pots on a bed of sawdust, and uses sawdust and scrap wood, with additions of seaweed, as the main fuel for the kiln.

BIN KILNS

These are made from metal dustbins or old oil drums. They are convenient containers for firing large single pots, although they can also be used for several pots at a time, if packed carefully.

Vinitha McWhinnie and her dustbin kiln

Gabriele Koch. *Round vessel, sawdust-fired in an old oil drum*

GABRIELE KOCH

Gabriele Koch uses an old oil drum and usually fires one piece at a time. She finds that the amount of sawdust surrounding the pot is important, and she ensures that there is a good thickness (about 18 cm [7in]) of sawdust above it. This serves not only to protect the pot from accidental contact with the flame of the blowtorch that Koch uses to ignite the kiln, but also to provide a good build-up of heat in the sawdust. This is essential to guarantee that smouldering continues right down to the bottom of the bin, and also to obtain interesting carbon markings.

Bin kilns usually have no air gaps in the walls. While this provides excellent protection from draughts, the lack of air towards the bottom of the bin means that the fire has to take a very good hold at the top to ensure complete combustion.

Bins are also used as reservoirs of fresh sawdust for the post-firing reduction of hot pots drawn from raku kilns. Anne James and David Roberts both use sawdust in this way.

Sawdust has become a popular fuel for carbonization and post-firing reduction

because it is available in large quantities, is easy to handle and is very cheap. Any other organic fuel, such as straw, pine needles or cow dung, could also serve to produce carbonization under properly controlled firing conditions.

Karin Hessenberg. *Porcelain alpaca.*
Sawdust-fired

CHAPTER NINE

RELATED FIRING TECHNIQUES

Many of the potters who have chosen to work with sawdust firing have done so because they are attracted by pots which are unglazed and fired in simple kilns. The technology may be straightforward, but making and firing these pots requires a high degree of skill and understanding of the materials.

There are many kinds of kiln in use around the world for which organic and surplus materials provide the fuel.

Facing page, from left to right:

A bonfiring. Pots made by Nigerian potters at the International Potters Camp, 1989, warming over hot embers from a previous firing

Wood and brush being packed around the warm pots

The burning bonfire

Right: *When the fire has burned out, the pots are revealed in the ashes. The fuel leaves carbon marks on the clay.* (Photograph by Robin Parrish)

BONFIRE AND OPEN-PIT KILNS

Probably the simplest types of kiln are bonfires and open pits. Some simple kilns can be regarded as hybrids of pits and bonfires.

Bonfire kilns are one of the oldest of all firing methods, and are still used in some parts of the world because of their speed and efficiency. Fuels include grass, wood and animal dung. Many finely decorated pots can be produced in these kilns if the pots are protected from direct contact with the fuel and the firing is carefully controlled to ensure even heating. Carbon marks on pots are caused by contact with burning fuel and are regarded by some potters, such as American Pueblo Indian potters, for example, as a fault which spoils the decoration. They produce pots with intricate and sophisticated designs, as shown on page 79. These designs would be seriously marred by carbon marks resulting from the firing.

A Pueblo Indian kiln is fired with dried cow dung, which is an ideal fuel because it burns slowly. A shallow hole is made on level ground to form the base of the kiln, and a wood fire is lit in the hole to dry the ground and to warm the pots, which are laid around it. When the embers have died down, a support for the pots is made on the ashes, using stones or an iron grate. Stones or a piece of tin cover the pots to protect them from the fire, and then dry cakes of cow dung are placed all round the pots. The potter knows how much fuel is required, and the colour of the pots indicates whether they have been fired sufficiently.

At San Ildefonso and Santa Clara in New Mexico, highly polished black pots are made. About half an hour before the end of the firing, the kiln is smothered with loose dung, causing smoke and carbonization. Maria Martinez is probably the most famous of the modern Pueblo potters producing black pots.

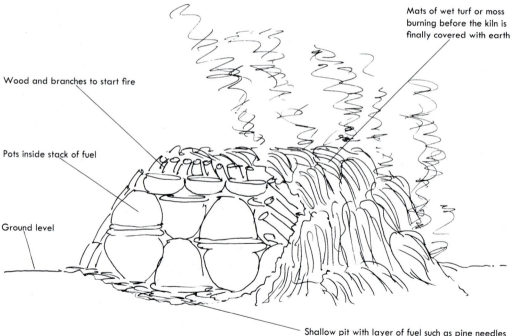

Mats of wet turf or moss burning before the kiln is finally covered with earth

Wood and branches to start fire

Pots inside stack of fuel

Ground level

Shallow pit with layer of fuel such as pine needles

Cut-away view of an open-pit kiln

A Pueblo painted pot from North America. These pots are protected from contact with the fuel during firing, so that carbon marks do not obscure the fine decoration. (Courtesy of the British Museum)

Maria Martinez. *Blackware jar. Height 17.8 cm (7 in).* (Courtesy of the National Museum of American Art, Smithsonian Institution, Gift of the IBM Corporation)

CLAMP KILNS

Pit or bonfire kilns which are smothered with damp fuel towards the end of the firing to produce carbonization are sometimes called clamp kilns.

Clamp kilns are still used in parts of Spain to produce black pots. In his book about traditional potteries in Spain and Portugal, Emili Sempere describes a kind of pit firing which is basically a type of clamp kiln. The survival of these kilns up to the present day is due to the exceptional qualities of thermal-shock resistance of the local granitic and ferruginous clays. Kilns of this type can be found at Fazamoes, in northern Portugal, and at Llamas de Mouro, Asturias, in north-west Spain.

A shallow pit is dug in the ground. This is roughly 3 metres (almost 10 ft) in diameter and about 50 cm (20 in) deep. The pots are stacked in the centre of the pit to form a truncated pyramid, which is about 1 metre (3 ft 4 in) in height.

Large pots are placed in the bottom part of the stack, with smaller pieces filling the gaps. The firing is started with pieces of wood, and when these are half burnt down the whole kiln is covered with mats of wet grass and moss. Once the grass cover has started burning, it maintains the temperature inside.

After about an hour, the pots are considered to be fired and the second phase begins. When the grass mats are half burnt away and the whole kiln is red-hot, the potter covers it with earth, using a hoe, and makes sure that every chink is completely sealed. This starts the process of reduction with a build-up of carbon monoxide, and this stage lasts approximately two hours.

ARNE BJORN (DENMARK)

Similar kilns have been excavated in Denmark, and the Danish potter Arne Bjorn describes how he reconstructed and fired two of these kilns.

For the simplest clamp kiln, Bjorn made a circular hollow in the ground, about 25 cm (10 in) deep and 75 cm (30 in) in diameter. The depth of the hollow was important, as a very shallow depression in the ground would have exposed the pots to too much draught and prevented effective reduction. The kiln required about a hundred blocks of turf to cover it. The fuel that he used was dry straw and 15 kg (33 lb) of very dry wood in 0.6 m (2 ft) lengths.

Bjorn filled the hollow with straw, and then laid in the bone-dry pots with their openings downwards. He stacked the wood up against the pots to form a wigwam shape about 75 cm (30 in) high. He placed a ring of turf around the base and ignited the straw. As soon as the wood was well alight, the turf was used to cover the kiln completely. A little ventilation was allowed at the bottom of the kiln.

Bjorn watched the kiln for five hours, and any gaps which appeared were filled with spare turf. After five hours, he filled all the cracks in the kiln with earth and sand. The kiln was left to cool until the next day, and then opened very slowly to avoid dunting of the pots.

Bjorn also constructed another kiln, which was a copy of a kiln excavated at Limhamn in northern Denmark. This was an improved version of the simple clamp, as it had underground channels for bringing air to the fire. The Limhamn kiln was capable of firing pots to a higher temperature than the simple clamp. It also fired very slowly and developed a good heat.

One underground channel acted as the firing channel, which led into the bottom of the kiln chamber. Bjorn placed a small quantity of kindling material, such as newspaper or straw, at the bottom of the kiln and then put a few kilograms of charcoal on top. He arranged a mix of pots and fuel wood on the charcoal until the heap was just above ground level.

Bjorn then covered the heap with turf and sand, leaving a small hole in order to check that the kiln was alight. He lit the fire by putting a taper of twisted paper into the fire channel. When smoke appeared from the checking hole left in the roof of the kiln, he sealed the fire channel with stones and clay.

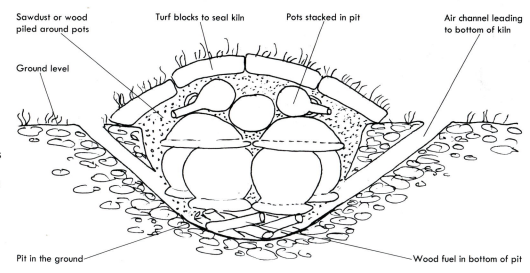

Sawdust or wood piled around pots

Turf blocks to seal kiln

Pots stacked in pit

Air channel leading to bottom of kiln

Ground level

Pit in the ground

Wood fuel in bottom of pit

A clamp kiln

He then sealed two of the air channels, and left the kiln to burn very slowly for about twenty-four hours.

David Harvey describes building a clamp kiln very similar to Arne Bjorn's Limhamn kiln. His kiln uses sawdust as a fuel, and is made in a shallow pit in the ground. Tubes leading to the base of the fire provide ventilation. Harvey lights the wood in the bottom before piling sawdust on top. Once the sawdust is smouldering, he beds pots into it and covers these with more sawdust, closing the top of the kiln with turf. The fire burns out after about fourteen hours.

The pots show a variety of grey, red, buff and black marks, where they have been exposed to variations in oxidizing and reducing atmospheres. Those pots near the vent on the windward side of the clamp receive more air and are partly oxidized, while those on the sheltered side are more heavily reduced. Harvey has found that pots fired in a clamp kiln are stronger than those fired in a simple sawdust kiln.

SOPHISTICATED KILNS

DAVID HARVEY

David Harvey's sophisticated sawdust kiln is designed to produce varied markings on pots through a controlled re-oxidation at the end of the firing.

He builds up the kiln in layers with pots supported on wire netting. He places ventilation tubes made from old clay or metal pipes in the kiln walls, and arranges fast-burning layers of wood shavings alternately with layers of slow-burning fine sawdust. This system produces strong contrasts of oxidized and reduced colour marks on the pots.

Harvey lights the kiln from the top, and then covers it with a dustbin lid. When the kiln is nearly burned down, he introduces some kindling wood at the bottom by removing a few loose bricks. He allows the wood to burn briskly, producing flames around the dustbin lid. He then leaves the kiln to cool before unpacking the pots.

ROMAN KILNS

Harvey goes on to describe a simple Roman kiln, which can be built by anyone willing to excavate a hole in the ground. The Roman kiln is basically an improved type of clamp kiln, being built in a pit and having a firing channel for the fuel. The main differences are the domed clay roof to the firing chamber and the floor supports, which are used to prevent pots coming into direct contact with the fuel. The clay roof can be built by packing soft clay on to an arched wicker framework of willow branches. The clay dome dries and fires hard when the kiln is fired.

Several experimental kilns made with willow and clay have been built and fired by Gerhild Tschachler-Nagy. She has described these kilns in her article in *Ceramic Review* magazine (see the Bibliography, page 94).

The kilns described so far in this chapter are simple structures with low firing temperatures. However, black or carbonized pots do not have to be fired in such simple kilns.

MOORISH-TYPE KILNS

In parts of Spain, black pottery is produced in kilns the size of a small house. There are potters making black ware in several towns and villages, such as Quart and Verdu in Catalonia, the region around Barcelona. Ramon Rabinat of Verdu, near Lerida, uses a large Moorish-type kiln to produce a range of traditional bottles, pitchers and jars.

The vessels intended for black firing are burnished lightly by polishing with a soft cloth at the leather-hard stage. The kiln has a large fire box beneath a perforated floor. This allows heat to circulate around the pots, which are stacked up in the main firing chamber. A Moorish kiln may have up to twelve vents or chimneys in the roof, and these multiple vents ensure good control of the firing. By covering and uncovering the vents, the potter can adjust the draught inside the kiln to ensure a good distribution of flames and heat across the firing chamber.

The fuel used is mainly wood: branches, brushwood and off-cuts from local carpenters' workshops. When the kiln has reached firing temperature, the potter covers all the vents with pieces of tile, and covers the roof of the kiln with sand and earth to seal it completely. The kiln is then stoked with small quantities of damp fuel to produce reduction. After a slow cooling period lasting for two or three days, the kiln is unpacked. The pots are black, with circular grey spots where they have touched in the stack.

Unglazed bottles keep water cool in the hot summer months through evaporation of the water, which seeps out of the minute pores in the clay. The black ware is thought to be more hygienic than other unglazed wares. The theory is that the carbon and other chemical changes in the clay produced by reduction act as a bactericide, and so keep the pores of the water bottles clean.

A botijo, or drinking-water bottle, made by Ramon Rabinat of Verdu, Catalonia. The pale grey spot on the black ground forms where the pots touch one another in the kiln pack. (Photograph by Stephen Brayne)

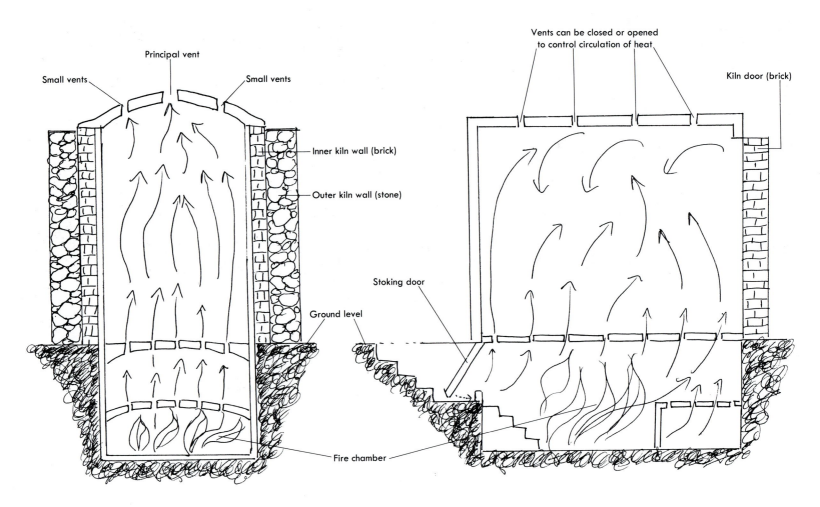

Principal vent

Small vents

Small vents

Vents can be closed or opened
to control circulation of heat

Kiln door (brick)

Inner kiln wall (brick)

Outer kiln wall (stone)

Stoking door

Ground level

Fire chamber

A Moorish-type kiln from Spain

A Moorish-type kiln at the pottery of Roca Caus in Verdu.
(Photograph by Robin Parrish)

The fuel store for a kiln in a Spanish pottery. The potters use all kinds of timber off-cuts, old furniture and sawdust

TECHNICAL NOTES

TIPS FOR SUCCESS WITH SAWDUST FIRING

1 The greatest risk in sawdust firing lies in the pots cracking during the heating or cooling of the kiln. This risk can be reduced in the following ways:

(**a**) Use a clay which is 'open'. The clay can be opened by the addition of grog, or by mixing the clay body with another grogged clay. Many of the potters mentioned in this book have found that a mixture of T-Material with porcelain or white stoneware makes a good combination of clays, as this is non-vitrified.

(**b**) Evenly constructed pot walls help to reduce thermal stress. Thin walls conduct heat better than thick walls, again reducing stress, but evenness is more important.

2 Ensure that the sawdust kiln heats up evenly. I do this by lighting the fire evenly round the top of the kiln. Other potters use a lid to prevent wind from fanning the flames. A pit kiln (see page 78) has no draughty gaps in the sides and conserves heat very well.

3 The biscuit temperature should be high enough to strengthen the clay body, but not so high as to cause the body to close and become dense. A dense body has a low resistance to thermal shock, while a body that is almost completely closed may not accept carbonization very well.

My attempts to sawdust fire porcelain which had previously been fired to above 1150°C (2102°F) resulted in greasy-looking brown smudges instead of rich blacks. This was because the heat produced in my sawdust kiln was too low for carbon to react with the almost vitrified clay. For carbonization to work on a vitrified body, it is necessary to sawdust fire at a high temperature – the method used by Joanna Constantinidis (see page 52), Byron Temple (see page 54) and John Leach (see page 57).

4 A burnished clay surface will accept and show up carbon marks more readily than an unburnished surface. White or red clays respond better than buff clays, which can give dull results.

Burnishing tools can be very simple. Old spoons, pebbles and pieces of polished wood all make good burnishing tools.

GREEK VASE PAINTING

Details of the methods of Greek vase painting have been described by Joseph Veach Noble in his book *The Techniques of Painted Attic Pottery* (see the Bibliography, page 94).

The Greeks had to take great care when painting their pots to achieve an even thickness of *terra sigillata* slip, so thick, concise brushwork was essential. The artist would have had to ensure that lines were well attached to the pot to prevent re-oxidation from underneath. Some Attic vases which were not painted carefully enough show reddish brush streaks in the black, where the *terra sigillata* was applied too thinly and has re-oxidized in the firing.

Veach Noble also describes the chemical reactions which take place in *terra sigillata* during the Ancient Greek firing cycle. In the reduction phase, carbon monoxide is produced instead of carbon dioxide because of incomplete combustion of the fuel:

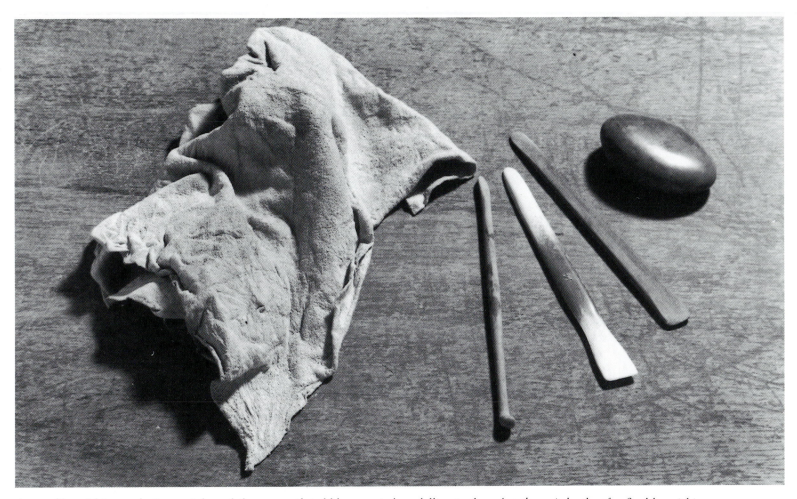

A set of burnishing tools. From right to left: a smooth pebble, assorted modelling tools and a chamois leather for final burnishing.
(Photograph by Stephen Brayne)

$$Fe_2O_3 + CO = \qquad 2FeO + CO_2$$
(Red iron oxide   (Black ferrous oxide)
in slip and clay)

The water vapour produced from the damp fuel or bowl of water produces magnetic iron oxide (Fe_3O_4), which is even blacker than ferrous iron oxide (FeO). The water may also assist the formation of blacks by lowering the firing temperature at which reactions take place. If the temperature rises to about 1050°C (1922°F), the black will re-oxidize to red.

Pot fragments illustrated in Veach Noble's book show how the Greeks fired and stoked their kilns.

CRISTOBALITE

Cristobalite is a crystalline from of quartz, and is produced when clay is heated above 900°C (1652°F). If cristobalite is present in a clay body after biscuit firing, it will help to reduce crazing in the glaze. Potters and manufacturers of ceramics exploit this property of quartz as a means of avoiding crazed glazes.

As the biscuit-firing temperature is increased, more quartz converts to cristobalite. The cristobalite content of the clay increases progressively as the temperature increases, up to about 1150°C (2102°F). Above this temperature, the cristobalite converts to another crystalline form of quartz called mullite. As cristobalite is the desirable crystalline form, the potter aims for the maximum biscuit temperature (usually about 1120°C [2048°F]) before the cristobalite turns to mullite.

On cooling, some of the cristobalite converts back to quartz at about 220°C (428°F), with a resulting shrinkage of the clay body. This is known as the 'cristobalite squeeze'. The clay body shrinks enough to allow for the glaze shrinkage after the glaze firing, and thus prevents crazing.

This is the principle that John Dermer (see page 43) applies to his work to prevent crazing in his *terra sigillata* slip.

HEALTH AND SAFETY

CERAMIC FIBRE
Great care should be taken when handling ceramic fibre, as it can be hazardous to health. Gloves, overalls and a good-quality dust mask suitable for use with ceramic fibre should be worn. It is particularly important to avoid breathing in fibres. Cheap fabric dust masks such as those obtainable in do-it-yourself stores are not adequate. In the UK, masks should conform to the relevant Euro Standard for toxic dusts: EN 143.

SMOKE
All sawdust kilns can be very smoky, so it is important to minimize the nuisance to neighbours and to comply with pollution-control regulations. Most urban areas in Britain are designated smoke-free zones, in which there may be restricted hours during which you can have a bonfire.

GLOSSARY

AGGREGATION The association of very small suspended particles to form clumps, which then settle out of the suspension.

ALKALINE EARTH Oxides of barium, calcium and magnesium.

BALL CLAY Any secondary clay which is very plastic.

BISCUIT FIRING Firing of clay to the point at which the clay is converted to ceramic, but remains porous.

BIZEN Region of Japan where pots are glazed by the action of flying wood ash in wood-fuelled kilns.

BODY STAINS Commercially prepared colours for colouring clay bodies or for use under glazes.

BURNISHING Polishing and compressing the surface of clay at the leather-hard stage to give a sheen in the biscuit-fired piece.

CALBRITE Fine ball-clay grog.

CALGON Commercial name for sodium hexametaphosphate used to prepare *terra sigillata*.

CARBONIZATION The blackening of clay by carbon trapped in the pores during sawdust or similar firing processes.

CLAMP KILN A type of pit kiln whose top is closed with turf or earth.

COLLOID Very small particles suspended in a liquid, giving a mixture with properties between those of a solution and a suspension.

CRISTOBALITE A crystalline form of quartz, which forms between 900–1150°C (1652–2102°F).

DEFLOCCULANT A substance, usually an alkali, which prevents suspended particles from aggregating.

DUNTING Cracking of fired pots by cooling down too rapidly or unevenly.

FINES Very fine particles in a solution, which take a long time to settle.

FLASHING Patches of colour variation on clay or glaze, caused by volatile oxides or contact with flame.

FLOCCULATION The aggregation of suspended particles to form clumps or flocs, which then settle out.

FLUX Metal oxide which acts as a melting agent for silica in a glaze.

FUMING The process whereby colours form on a clay surface due to the vaporization of volatile salts and oxides.

GREENWARE Unfired dry clay pots.

GROG Fired clay which has been ground to grains or dust. It is added to fine clays to improve their structure.

HAKE BRUSH A type of flat Japanese brush, used for applying slip to pots.

ION An atom which has acquired a positive or negative charge through the gain or loss of electrons.

KIDNEY A kidney-shaped tool, normally made of rubber or metal shim, which is used for smoothing and scraping the clay surface.

KILN PUTTY A thick paste of refractory material used for sealing gaps in kiln bricks.

KILN WASH A thin mix of water and refractory materials used to coat kiln shelves to prevent pots from sticking to them.

LEATHER-HARD The point at which unfired clay is very stiff, but not completely dry.

LEVIGATED SLIP A slip of very fine clay particles made by suspending them in large volumes of water. An alkali is often used to aid suspension.

LUSTRE The metallic surface on a glaze produced by firing appropriate mixtures of metal oxides on to the pot.

MATURING TEMPERATURE The temperature at which a glaze melts or clay vitrifies.

MUFFLE KILN A gas, oil or wood-fired kiln with a complete inner wall, which prevents flames from coming into contact with pots.

OXIDATION (OXIDIZING FIRING) Firing conditions with plenty of air to provide oxygen. Resulting glaze and clay colours are different from those fired in reducing conditions.

PIT KILN A kiln built in a shallow hole in the ground.

PORCELAIN A type of very white clay which is translucent at high temperatures. It contains a high proportion of pure china clay, feldspar and quartz. The clay body can be used at low temperatures for a fine white body.

POST-FIRING REDUCTION Reducing glazes and clay bodies after a firing process by means of combustible matter such as sawdust. Post-reduction following on raku firing results in various effects, such as a blackened body and crackle glazes.

PROP A support for kiln shelves made from refractory clay.

RAKU A Japanese firing process in which glazed pots are drawn hot from the kiln and plunged into a container of combustible material to alter the colour of the clay and glaze.

REDUCING AGENT A substance which will remove chemically combined oxygen from clay or glaze to alter the colour.

REDUCTION FIRING Firing which takes place with insufficient air, so that chemically-combined oxygen is drawn out of clay and glaze to maintain combustion. This produces characteristic colours in clay and glaze which are different from those fired in oxidizing conditions.

REFRACTORY CLAY A type of clay which is highly resistant to the effects of heat and repeated firings.

RESIST A substance which is used to prevent glaze, slip or carbon from reaching the underlying clay or glaze surface.

SAGGAR A container, usually made from a refractory clay, which is used to protect pots from flames inside a kiln.

SETTER Kiln furniture designed to support individual pieces of ware.

SINTERING The point at which a glaze fuses to the clay pot but has not yet melted.

TANNING ACTION The action of tannic acid or natural tannins as curing agents. The curing of hides to produce leather is an example.

TEMPER Material added to clay to improve its resistance to thermal shock.

TERRA SIGILLATA Slip made from very fine clay particles which has a very smooth, lustrous surface.

THERMAL SHOCK Cracking of pots due to rapid heating or cooling.

T-MATERIAL Type of grogged white stoneware suitable for making sculptures or large pots.

TOP-HAT KILN A kiln in the form of a top hat, which is placed over the pots to be fired. The kiln is lifted on to or off a base by means of a hoist. This enables single, large pieces to be raku-fired.

UNDERGLAZE Commercially prepared colours for use under the glaze on a pot.

VAPORIZATION (VOLATILIZATION) The point at which a metal oxide or salt becomes a gas due to the effect of heat.

VERMICULITE A micaceous mineral used as an insulator in kilns and furnaces.

VITRIFICATION The point at which impurities in clay melt and fill the pores with glassy material.

Karin Hessenberg dusting ash off a bridge pot. (Photograph by Stephen Brayne)

LIST OF SUPPLIERS

UK

Acme Marls Ltd
Bournes Bank
Burslem
Stoke-on-Trent ST6 3DW
(*Saggars, kiln furniture, fireclays*)

Morgan Refractories Ltd
Liverpool Road
Neston
South Wirral
Cheshire L64 3RE
(*T-Material*)

Potclays Ltd
Brickkiln Lane
Etruria
Stoke-on-Trent

Potterycrafts Ltd
Campbell Road
Shelton

AUSTRALIA

Ceramic Supply Co.
61 Lakemba Street
Belmore
NSW 2192

Diamond Ceramic Supplies Ltd
50–52 Geddes Street
Mulgrave
Melbourne
Victoria 3170

Walker Ceramics
Boronia Road
Wantirna
Victoria
PO Box 208
Bayswater 3153

USA

Ceramic Supply of New York and New
Jersey
7 Route 46 West
Lodi
NJ 07644

Continental Clay Company
1101 Stenson Boulevard NE
Minneapolis
MN 55413

Del-Val Potters Supply Co.
7600 Queen Street
Wyndmoor
PA 19118

Ferro Corporation
PO Box 6650
Cleveland
Ohio 44101

BIBLIOGRAPHY

PREFACE AND CHAPTER 1
Birks, Tony 'David Roberts – Raku, 1990' (The Craft Centre and Design Gallery, Leeds, 1990)
Brisson, Harriet *Ceramic Review* (Issue no. 71, 1981)
Cooper, Emmanuel *A History of World Pottery* (B.T. Batsford, 1988)
Flight, Graham *Ceramics Manual* (HarperCollins, 1990)
Soldner, Paul *Ceramic Review* (Issue no. 124, 1990)

CHAPTER 2
Cooper, Emmanuel and Frankel, Cyril 'Gabriele Koch, 1989' (The Craft Centre and Design Gallery, Leeds, 1989)
Queensberry, David 'Magdalene Odundo', *Neue Keramik* (Issue no. 2, 1992)
Salmon, Antonia *Ceramic Review* (Issue no. 130, 1991)

CHAPTER 3
Clinton, Margery *The Complete Potter: Lustres* (B.T. Batsford, 1991)

Cooper, Emmanuel 'Karin Hessenberg – Fire and Form, 1988' (The Craft Centre and Design Gallery, Leeds, 1988)
Leach, Bernard *A Potter's Book* (Faber & Faber, 1969)
—*The Art of Bernard Leach* (Exhibition catalogue, Asahi Shimbun, 1980)
Trim, Judy *Ceramic Review* (Issue no. 102, 1986)
Varley, Sue *Ceramic Review* (Issue no. 92, 1985)

CHAPTER 4
Bayle, Pierre *Ceramic Review* (Issue no. 121, 1990)
— *La Revue de la Céramique et du Verre* (Issue no. 63, 1992)
Cooper, Emmanuel 'Duncan Ross, 1991' (The Crafts Centre and Design Gallery, Leeds, 1991)
Cooper, Emmanuel and Royle, Derek *Glazes for the Studio Potter* (B.T. Batsford, 1978)
Dermer, John *Ceramics Art and Perception* (Issue no. 4, 1991)
—'Burnt Earth – The Journey' (BHP Minerals, 1992)

Emmins, Jane 'Terra-raku-lata' *Ceramic Review* (Issue no. 137, 1992)
Gibson, John *Pottery Decoration* (A & C Black, 1987)
Green, David *A Handbook of Pottery Glazes* (Faber & Faber, 1978)
Lane, Arthur *Greek Pottery* (Faber & Faber, 1947)
Rhodes, Daniel *Clay and Glazes for the Potter* (Pitman, 1965)
Ross, Duncan *Ceramic Review* (Issue no. 129, 1991)
Salazar, Fiona *Crafts* (Issue no. 74, 1985)
—*Ceramic Review* (Issue no. 107, 1987)
Veach Noble, Joseph *The Techniques of Painted Attic Pottery* (Faber & Faber, 1966)
Winter, Adam 'Terra Sigillata', *Neue Keramik* (Issue no. 2, 1992)

CHAPTER 5
Allan, Ruth *Ceramics Monthly* (January 1992)
Gibbs, Peter *New Zealand Potter* (Issue no. 1, 1986)

Hayes, Barry *Ceramic Review* (Issue no. 117, 1989)

CHAPTER 6
Allan, Ruth *Ceramics Monthly* (January 1992)
Dermer, John *Ceramics Art and Perception* (Issue no. 4, 1991)
Leach, John *Ceramic Review* (Issue no. 67, 1981)
—*Ceramic Review* (Issue no. 115, 1989)
Temple, Byron *Ceramic Review* (Issue no. 78, 1982)
—*Ceramics Art and Perception* (Issue no. 6, 1991)

CHAPTER 7
Branfman, Steven *Raku* (A & C Black, 1991)
Byers, Ian *The Complete Potter: Raku* (B.T. Batsford, 1990)
Perryman, Jane *Ceramic Review* (Issue no. 122, 1990)

Roberts, David *Ceramic Review* (Issue no. 137, 1992)

CHAPTER 8
Gibbs, Peter *New Zealand Potter* (Issue no. 1, 1986)
Hayes, Barry *Ceramic Review* (Issue no. 117, 1989)
Trim, Judy *Ceramic Review* (Issue no. 102, 1986)

CHAPTER 9
Barry, John W. *American Indian Pottery* (Books Americana, 1981)
Barry, Val 'Pueblo Pots', *Ceramic Review* (Issue no. 28, 1974)
Bjorn, Arne *Man, Fire and Clay through the Ages* (Van Nostrand Rheinhold, 1969)
Blandino, Betty *Coiled Pottery* (A & C Black, 1984)
Harvey, David *Imaginative Pottery* (Pitman, 1976)

Llorens Artigas, J. and Corredor-Matheos, J. *Ceramica Popular Española* (Editorial Blume, 1982)
Martinez, Maria *Ceramic Review* (Issue no. 68, 1981)
'Nigerian and Kenyan Pottery' *Crafts* (Issue no. 101, 1989)
Riegger, Hal *Primitive Pottery* (Van Nostrand Rheinhold, 1972)
Sempere, Emili *Rutas a los Alfares* (Barcelona, 1982)
Tschachler-Nagy, Gerhild 'Kilns', *Ceramic Review* (Issue no. 138, 1992)

TECHNICAL NOTES
Veach Noble, Joseph *The Techniques of Painted Attic Pottery* (Faber & Faber, 1966)

INDEX